# Disclaimer

Nothing stated or presented in this book is intended to be a substitute for professional medical advice, diagnosis, or treatment. Always seek the advice of your physician or other qualified healthcare provider if you have any questions regarding a medical condition, diet, nutritional supplementation, exercise regimen, or any other matter related to your health and well-being. All information provided in this book is simply based on the author's experience.

# LOVE
## MANIFESTS
# FORM

GUIDANCE FOR CULTIVATING CONSCIOUS
EVOLUTION THROUGH THE VEHICLE OF LOVE

## Tova Sardot, PhD

Love Manifests Form

Guidance for Cultivating Conscious Evolution
through the Vehicle of Love

Copyright © 2024 Tova Sardot, PhD

Book Design by
Transcendent Publishing

ISBN: 979-8-9900956-1-8

Printed in the United States of America.

# Acknowledgments

I have deep gratitude for all the friends and colleagues who have read, critiqued, and offered other assistance for this book:

- Stuart Sovatsky, PhD
- Cody Golman, DC
- Arjuna
- Stacy Claxton
- Drew Jackson
- Jesse and Catherine

You all helped make this project possible, and I have so much admiration for each of your strengths and superpowers. I feel fortunate to be surrounded by such talent and connection.

For the cover art, I would like to acknowledge the inspiring artwork of Nicolas Kristen-Honshin. I was in Sedona at his studio in 2023, and one of his paintings with pairs of mirrored hummingbirds brought me to tears. My response was an intuitive signal that it must somehow be part of this book. I was fortunate to meet and speak with Honshin at his studio, and he is an endlessly delightful human. His artwork is magic and transports you to the depths of your soul and unspoken truths. He can point to what I write about in hundreds of pages in one painting. His work is transformative.

Here is Honshin's description of hummingbirds in his art: "The hummingbird is a symbol of levity, ascending energy, and the divine of gravity, and in this way, it is the symbol of the ultimate alchemist in nature. The hummingbird represents the aware consciousness that emerges and gathers nectar. This nectar symbolizes love, compassion, joy, forgiveness, and equanimity. The hummingbird's intention in collecting this nectar is to share it with all the suffering hearts that all beings may end suffering. The antidote for suffering is what the hummingbird offers: love, compassion, peace, and kindness."

The hummingbird is the mascot of our work together in this spirit!

# Table of Contents

# Journey to This Moment

People often wonder how I got into spirituality after spending much of my life in research science. For me, this book is the culmination of a phase of my life and my work on the planet, where the story of who I was before now matters less. However, I'm including it here as helpful background for the curious.

I have always been drawn to science and earned a bachelor's degree in physics and a doctorate in chemistry. There is a lot to love about learning and understanding the world around me, but it wasn't until graduate school that I was drawn to utilizing my expertise to help the environment of our planet.

My dissertation focused on recycling industrial waste to lower pollution rates and address the increasing problem of overfilled landfills in American cities and worldwide. After graduate school, I went on to work in bioplastics, only to be disenchanted by the corporate world's endless desire for money, power, and more of it. Then, I was awarded a fellowship to work at the Environmental Protection Agency (EPA) in Washington, DC.

There, I was sure I would find like minds and the ability to make environmental policy change backed by science. During my time at the EPA, I did find like-minded colleagues. However, many had already been soured by countless years in a system where scientifically backed change was irreversibly politicized.

You had to learn to "play the game" and navigate the politics. Well, that's precisely what snuffs the spark in people who want to make change through the government albatross. In time, I realized I was brought through these experiences to learn that what I thought I wanted to do (driven by the left side of the brain and ego) was not my actual purpose in life.

I don't say this to minimize the importance of my time at the EPA—I needed to experience that time to understand what would come next. In my first year there, I began having increasing symptoms of chronic illness that doctors couldn't find the source of.

In my second year at EPA, I was *really* struggling. The brain fog, insomnia, and fatigue were so bad that, on many days, I couldn't remember my phone number. My quality of life was dwindling, and I needed answers. I had a friend who had gone to a treatment clinic in Switzerland for a chronic illness and experienced great results. Desperate to find guidance, I decided to make the same journey.

Switzerland was a huge turning point for me in my health and career. The doctor I worked with at the clinic was able to identify that the core of my issue was Lyme disease, and they treated me for three weeks. When I returned home, I was beginning to feel better, but it would take over two more years of supplement protocols and many treatments to heal.

At that, I plateaued until I started focusing on the emotional component of the illness. Later, I realized that when we are beginning to set foot on our path, it is common to experience illness, accidents, or significant losses that allow us an entry point for our spiritual growth.

When my EPA fellowship ended, I was looking for my next career move and knew I wanted to move back home, back out west. I was offered a job at an EPA research facility in Denver. Although I debated whether it was the right move for me, my intuition told me, *If you want to help the planet, help the individual people.*

My intuition went on to describe how when people have a chaotic mind and no access to their body and higher consciousness, they can't make decisions that ultimately serve the planet or themselves. This was a massive awakening for me, reflecting on what I was to work on personally and the best way to focus my efforts to help others.

After this awareness and my experience in Switzerland, I declined the EPA position and completely changed my life. I started a master's program in complementary alternative medicine (CAM). I also mentored with multiple excellent medical doctors, including Dr. Dietrich Klinghardt.

I'll admit I left something out of the story. In my mid-twenties, while I was in school learning physics, I began seeing an intuitive healer in Los Angeles. Her work had so many implications for the reality we live in and the unseen energies around us beyond ordinary perception. At the time, I did not see how this correlated with the physics principles I was learning. It all sounded like magic from the perspective of academia and accepted science.

The concepts, however, stayed with me, and I went on to learn energy modalities like ThetaHealing, Holographic Healing, and BodyTalk. I practiced these on the down-low, as I identified as a scientist and felt the world would not take me seriously if they knew.

During this time, I finally began to understand that magic was simply science that was not yet understood. Further, it was beginning to become clear that the physics I learned in my twenties was mirroring the energetic modalities I was now studying.

Fast-forward to receiving my CAM master's degree, after which I worked at a naturopathic clinic, melding my learnings with subtle energy work. At this point, my energy work had morphed into my own "sauce" based on concepts from my training and intuitive information I had received for almost twenty years.

This book represents all that work in one place, plus its most recent advancements. Excitedly, I invite you to experience your own journey through this opening in conscious evolution.

# Prologue

You are at the beginning of one of countless journeys in your life. One of the evolutions of yourself within this specific human experience occurring through your ancestral lineage and many lives throughout your spiritual existence. This is an important concept to apply to your life: you exist beyond this particular human experience. You may enjoy and identify with your current human form, but when you die and leave this body, the expanded part of you will move on with all the growth you've accomplished in this life.

> *This is not to minimize the importance of the body. It is the precious vehicle through which all your experiences and growth are possible. The body is your sacred material form; when we treat it as such, its full technology opens up!*

We will explore the importance of hormones and this body technology in future chapters, as well as easy movement to engage with to optimize the physical being. Nutrition is another critical aspect of optimizing your body's technology. I will offer brief perspectives and direction on the topic, although it is not a main focus of this book.

You are indeed what you eat. Choosing quality food, eating with the season, and building an intuitive relationship with your body's needs are all essential aspects. When we are eating without awareness, our body is sluggish and stuck. Fad diets remove necessary nutrients. Even eating aligned with your culture can limit your body's hardware.

> *By mastering your body's inputs, you open the access of your cells to further evolutions. It makes all subsequent expansions easier.*

The purpose of this proficiency is not to limit yourself or suffer. On the contrary, it is to enjoy food and eat consciously. This means eating *with* your body and providing what it needs. We are here to enjoy being human; a big part of that experience is through this amazing physical vehicle.

The most beautiful and elegant system of nutrition that treats food as medicine comes from the five-thousand-year-old practice of Ayurveda. In Sanskrit, the word translates to "science of life." The practice covers more than just diet but includes extensive guidance on what to eat to create health in the body.

This system is a fantastic place to start to help you better understand your body and its needs. This understanding opens the communication between your body and mind, which leads to more profound intuition. Like all practices suggested in this book, Ayurveda is offered as a scaffolding to get you started. At some point, you will attain proficiency in food inputs and create your own ways of nourishing yourself with mastery.

Here, I will provide a short overview of the most fundamental concepts in Ayurveda. In this system, each person has a *dosha type* that personalizes their diet. Primarily, a person is either *vata, pitta,* or *kapha* based on their mental and emotional tendencies and the presentation of their physical form. Each of these corresponds to the basic body types: ectomorph (*vata*), mesomorph (*pitta*), and endomorph (*kapha*).

Further, the seasons are associated with the different *doshas.* When you are in the season corresponding to your *dosha*, there are some shifts to make so that energy does not build up. For example, I am mainly *kapha*, which corresponds to winter. *Kapha* is heavy, wet, and oily by nature. If I eat foods that are also heavy, wet, or oily (like fats and squash), then I will feel extra sluggish and tired during the winter.

In this way, Ayurveda is the perfect system to help people understand themselves and their body's needs throughout the year. This dietary path supports feeling more energetic, improves brain clarity, and sets you up for overall health. All of this, in turn, gives you more access to the technology of your human body to make expansion and evolution occur more easily.

Eating in line with your *dosha* and the seasons is one of the most important supplementary tools of the journey laid out in this book. It may seem like a lot to take on at first, but you'll find yourself in the groove after four to six weeks and know what your body needs to thrive.

It is always a process, but it becomes easier to stick with it and feel the difference in how your body operates when you are eating in harmony with your natural tendencies. Then, you will notice what happens when you fall off that wagon, which is also crucial. Being more intentional with what you eat adds to your development of intuition, connecting you more deeply with your body and all the signals it uses to communicate its needs.

Many quizzes online can help you determine your primary *dosha type*, and many people also have a secondary type. There are also countless books on the system of Ayurveda and recipes. A few are mentioned in the "Suggested Resources" section at the end of this book. The easiest way to grasp the basics of this methodology and how it applies to you is to schedule a session with an Ayurvedic practitioner. This is my strong suggestion to get you started to eat in line with your deepest physical nature.

Here are Ayurvedic practitioners that I recommend:

- Dr. Leviyah Kern
  EarthsidePerpetualMedicine.com
  406-697-4984
  leviyahkern@gmail.com
- Stacy Claxton
  SoulsInSynergy.com
  stacy@soulsinsynergy.com

For many, this is an opportunity to resolve the struggle they experience due to eating foods out of coherence with them. You can see how this aids the optimization of the body as a fundamental piece in your evolution in consciousness. Let's continue to bring awareness and presence to all that we do. The goal is to align more deeply with harmony in ourselves and the natural world, which we often forget we are a part of.

# Introduction

Welcome to your evolution in consciousness! This book aims to help you:

- Shift perspectives that create flexibility in the mind to better comprehend your own reality and what you create.
- Understand hormones and their true purpose in health and your continued evolution.
- Develop an expanded experience of life through a deeper embodiment of yourself and connection to others while releasing blockages and density.
- Gain access to both sides of your brain and your heart space.
- Fully self-integrate and attain a maturation in life through the lens of Love.

Maturation is an upgraded human experience available for everyone—a self-mastery evolution of consciousness simply waiting for us to engage with it. This concept is based on the work of Stuart Sovatsky, whom we will meet in a later chapter.

## Impetus

Important insights can come to us in a flash. Unexpectedly, your understanding is permanently shifted in an instant. Does this sensation sound familiar to you? It is to me. In September of 2022, while in meditation, I suddenly and deeply understood that all human experience occurs either from a state of love or out of a state of separation. Part of me understood this before, but in that moment, a deeper knowing came that was so much more profound.

Over the next few days, I turned this knowing into a practice that, when done with intent and consciousness, can illuminate what often goes unseen. In my practice, I watched myself interact with others and the world and asked, "Am I in love or separation?" It became a fascinating and valuable practice that could unveil things I had not seen. I had considered myself somewhat aware of my ego and the tricks it played, as I had focused on building this awareness. However, with this simple practice, I could perceive some of the deeper patterns I had become accustomed to, which were so ingrained that I was blind to them. A deeper layer had emerged.

As I continued to interact with others, I also began asking if those I encountered came from a place of love or separation. Not out of judgment, of course: I wasn't taking note to tell them or try to "help." I took notice for myself and held space for the separate experiences of others. In essence, I worked to grow a specific awareness of what I was experiencing to watch the exchange from an outside perspective (much like what we will do in the "Watching the Thinker" exercise in chapter 2, but I have taken a step further in interactions with others).

A week after this eye-opening practice, I again received intuitive information in another meditation. This time, I learned I would write a book on love! While this message was a surprise, it was also to my dismay. Just two weeks prior, I had finished a chapter for a practitioner compilation book, and I had sworn I could never write an entire book alone.

Never say never, though, right? Although I was excited to be part of the previous book, the deadline was quick and required much time spent writing from the left side of my brain to finish. However, I knew that *this* book would be written differently. I would learn to allow the information to come through intuitively rather than forcing it.

Then information came bursting like popcorn, with pops of awareness and information. By then, I was getting excited about the project. I was all in! My practice of identifying love and separation had been illuminating for me, and I could sense this journey had so much in store for my development and future readers. Boy, was that an understatement!

## The Journey Ahead

Think of this book as a map of perspectives and practices we will explore together. These ways of working with people have come to me intuitively for almost twenty years, alongside my learnings from others through training, books, and professional friendships. All this is being brought together for the first time through the lens of Love—the force that brings all creation together.

> *The main goal of this book is to help you engage with the current evolution in consciousness to meet your true potential.*

I want to describe the origins of my perception of reality that comprise this book. The roots can be found at the intersection of science, research, observation, and intuition. Although I use citations in some sections, much of this book has been formed from my perception and informed by the collective unconscious. My perception is always trying to evolve and grow.

You are, of course, welcome to have whatever perception of reality you would like. This is part of the beauty of this experience—how different perspectives all contain a piece of the truth. No one human has all the answers. This is just as we are all pieces of God. For me, growing into an evolved perception of Love within and outside myself has changed everything for the better.

Through my journey, an ease began entering my life, one that was always right there but just out of reach. When you feel this ease enter on the waves of Love, you can step more deeply into the creatorship in your life. Living from this internal space brings expanded possibilities, joy, fulfillment, and happiness.

This higher state positively permeates everything in your life. It is different from loving yourself (which is a part of this journey); in fact, it is *being* Love—the Love that is at the core of each person but gets diluted with perceptions of self, difficult life experiences, societal expectations, and more. It is important to remember that everything we will do in this book is an activation, opening you more deeply to who you are. You already contain everything you need!

When you can show up as or in the frequency of Love, you become a manifesting magnet for what you want to create. You feel a new depth of gratification in every experience. Everyone has had glimpses of this. For example, it is easy to connect with nature through the feeling of awe. Likewise, when you spend time with a baby or children, their presence may connect you with the purity and awe of creation. By traveling the path of this book, feelings like awe, gratitude, and compassion become increasingly accessible and open the ability to consciously create your reality.

You will notice in this book that the word *love* will sometimes be capitalized and other times not. When *love* is lowercase, we refer to human love, whether romantic, platonic, or familial. This love has evolved out of necessity to continue our species—what's established within the family unit and community to improve survival. This type of love is mostly what is researched, experienced, and understood in our society.

Capital-letter Love, however, is an expanded version that encompasses deeper truths about who we are beyond the human experience and form. The beauty is that we are both human love and the more expanded, all-encompassing Love simultaneously! Because we are both human and spirit, our experience extends beyond this particular lifetime.

There are profound limitations to what our society considers science and currently accepted scientific thinking. Science is truly only as good as the consciousness conducting it, meaning that the observer will always affect the outcome of an experiment. This is an accepted principle of quantum mechanics, which describes reality's most fundamental inner workings.

Most current science assumes that the observer is separate from their experiments. However, there is interaction at subtle levels that are not considered. This is because sense perceptions, belief systems, and level of consciousness limit all human observations. You cannot truly be an objective observer. Consciousness so strongly influences your reality that it creates your perception and affects what occurs.

The scientists who have made some of the most impactful contributions and observations of our unseen reality, like Albert Einstein and Nikola Tesla, had a consciousness with access beyond our traditional five senses. Many other less well-known people also hold a connection to expanded places in the same way, whether they were aware of the information's source or not.

Expanded consciousness is a core concept in this book because it implies using your individual awareness to understand your broader reality. We first will consider what science says about where we are and how we got here. This follows mental evolution and primes you for more. Then we have context to truly understand the greater purpose of the heart and Love in our evolution.

The information for this book came in pieces, and I put it together like a puzzle to make sense of it for myself and, more importantly, for you! By the time I was writing chapter 5, I realized the chapters correlated with chakras. This book will take you through chakras 1 through 4 to purify and align your mental, emotional, and physical being and help you more fully embody your heart.

Although there will be subsequent books, it is unclear whether the next book will be in direct succession to this one. The idea is that through this book, you will establish enough capacity to continue the activations of the chakras from the throat through the crown on your own. What is most important is that we must have the alignment of the first four chakras before we can activate the ascending ones. This book aims to meet the initiate at their current level with the introduction of minimal esoteric knowledge.

If you are unfamiliar with the system of chakras, they are energy centers that were first described in Hindu Vedic texts many thousands of years ago. Chakras are subtle, unseen parts of the energetic body that contain emotional, psychological, and other physical-based energies and information.

If you are curious to learn more, there is a wealth of easily accessible information on chakras online, much of which is beyond the scope of this book. Each chapter also briefly describes how the material correlates with a chakra while also providing expansion practices that work with each chakra as part of a daily meditation exercise.

Some believe that we are currently expanding access from the solar plexus deeper into the heart chakra. This is why we find ourselves in a world where the sense of individual self has become well-developed.

This is not necessarily a bad thing, it is just our current stage in our evolution, as we will see.

When consciousness fully integrates within a chakra, a deeper activation occurs. This allows greater access to stability around its themes and the expanded awareness that comes with each successive chakra.

This current expansion is available for all of humanity. Are you ready to activate it?

## How to Use This Book

*The real secret of life is to be completely engaged with what you are doing . . . and instead of calling it work, realize it is play.*

—Alan Watts

This quote by Alan Watts truly is the secret to life. As you explore what this book offers, remember that you are a conscious being incarnated in a human body, playing and working to evolve yourself. Some may emphasize the more serious connotation of the word *work*. I, however, invite you to use the words *work* and *play* interchangeably.

Give yourself grace if some material comes less easily than others or if you need more time with exercises. Changing a pattern takes four to six weeks, so go easy on yourself and enjoy each stage of the journey. There is no destination, only the experience. If you keep your curiosity and playfulness with this process, it will be more enjoyable.

Conscious evolution is what this book is moving you toward and refers to the ability of an individual, group, or entire society to be purposeful participants in their betterment. This contrasts with biological evolution, which requires long periods to create change that positively influences the progress of a population.

Shifting mental concepts and committing to the exercises can be challenging and requires both time and dedication. Although this is the most important foundational work, this is also why every other chapter focuses on helping you develop practices to instill the ideas presented in your daily life. These chapters aim to help you apply and integrate information and prime you for progress throughout this book and beyond.

> *You are not doing the work if you don't apply the concepts to your life.*

You can see a video demonstration for many practices in this book on my YouTube channel, Tova Sardot.

> *One of this book's primary purposes is to guide you to fully integrate the self by balancing your internal density. This density takes on the form of stuck emotions, beliefs, or ways of perceiving reality.*

We will focus on chakra development because these are the centers that transmute emotions into energy for you and your interaction with the world. When these energy centers have been blocked by density from human experiences, there can be neither full activation nor adequate flow between them. In other words, your human self's complete physical, mental, and emotional technology is not working efficiently.

> *The human body is a technology of evolution.*

We will be awakening and purifying your energy centers. This occurs when you create a relationship with each chakra, implement practices to open them, and clarify the emotional and mental densities you find. We are working toward each chakra's stable openness and flow.

I strongly suggest you engage in these practices daily to make further development more effortless. Your commitment will be rewarded with the flowering of your being as you progress through this book and toward increased self-awareness and perspective shifts that lead to new ways of showing up in the world.

You will notice critical recurring themes and *many* check-ins throughout. This is to engage your mind at different stages of your evolution and stimulate new facets of awareness. When concepts are revisited, consider them an invitation to feel more profoundly into the concept to discover what new truths await.

It's important to note that your potential won't be able to bloom more if you skip steps along this journey. You may find yourself needing to return to themes multiple times to embody them fully. This can be frustrating and detouring. However, if you take your time and progress after attaining the levels of self-mastery, you will achieve greater and deeper progress overall.

Each perspective and exercise build a foundation that culminates in a final practice of this book: Your Inner Heart Union. Suppose you truly do the work throughout this book and make all the shifts; the Inner Heart Union will be an exceptionally impactful event for you. You will experience the evolution in consciousness that the planet is working toward right now.

## Additional Guidance

*My primary focus in writing this book is to create a guide for my clients that offers support throughout the programs I offer. At the same time, I have made it malleable enough for general consumption. Consider it a hybrid between a regular book and a workbook that should be approached more as if taking a class than simply absorbing information. Similar to when you take a class, concepts are repeated multiple times and in different contexts. The material is aimed at meeting near beginners to the moderately spiritually experienced. It is written to you and for you.*

There are also different individual interactions possible with the material presented here; you can consume every word and shift your reality, or maybe there is one sentence that brings you essential insight. There is no wrong way to interact with the information you find here because living your individual perspective is one of the most critical parts of your experience.

Beyond that, there is no right or wrong timing to evolve. Be gentle with yourself—it is not a race. One of the most comforting things to know is that it is easier than ever to make these leaps in consciousness because more people than ever in history have bushwhacked a path for us. In fact, as I finish writing this book, the path is already lifting and opening significantly more. This means that these evolutions will manifest faster and easier. Yet, it will always take awareness and commitment.

In many spiritual communities, there have been whispers of a Love wave that will bathe the Earth and activate the entire planet as part of our evolution. I do not know whether this is true or not. What I do know is that you can activate this on your own. One way is through the processes offered in this book; each person who accomplishes this will make it easier for others to do the same.

If the Love wave does come and you are already activated, you will have less difficulty assimilating because you have already cleared your density. For others, it will be like processing this book's practices in a moment, which could be quite jarring if the internal foundation hasn't been laid. With the powerful expansions currently occurring, you have more support than ever to make this evolution!

Regardless of what the future holds, let's start now and become a beacon of Love on the planet!

Before we dive in, I want to cover one more important concept. The Map Through the Journey picture below shows the relationship between concentric circles and a spiral path, one of our most natural forms. This shape is ubiquitous throughout nature—simply look at the Fibonacci sequence. Don't forget you are part of that exact nature; your ear, fisted hand, and DNA are a few examples of human body spirals.

Our own individual internal and spiritual evolutions also follow a spiral path. We may only notice our growth when we feel a plateau or return to old patterns, but it's an evolving spiral. Have you ever felt as if you had accomplished a lot and moved far ahead, only to feel you backtracked and lost all clarity suddenly?

I encourage you to remember the spiral path and that often, when you feel as though you're bumping up against old patterns, you have actually emerged at a higher octave of your evolution. 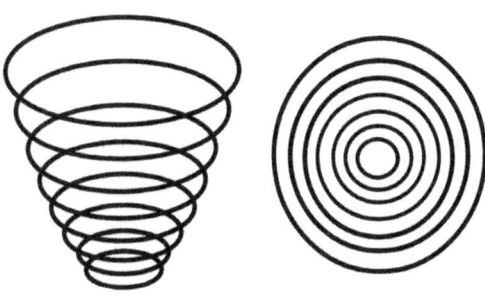 Being on the spiral but at a higher ring may correlate with an old theme coming back around so that you can either prove your mastery or work deeper on the pattern. Often, this is an expanded perception that has opened for you. Don't miss the opportunity, or let this discourage you. Continue on!

There are countless paths through the current evolution we find ourselves in. Many are saying similar things, just shared uniquely through an individual perspective. If you are reading this book, then the perspective I present likely resonates with you. If you find that it does not, then there are more paths than you can imagine.

# Map through the Journey

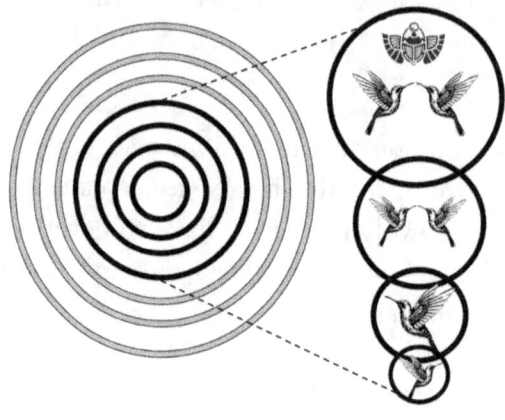

Chapter 9 &10
Love Manifests Form
Heart Chakra

Chapter 7 & 8
From Mind to Heart
Solar Plexus into Heart Chakra

Chapter 5 & 6
Evolution of the Brain & Mind
Solar Plexus Chakra

Chapter 3-4
Your Emotional Technology
Sacral Chakra

Chapter 1-2
Evolution of Hormones & Love
Root Chakra

The graphic above shows a map of our evolutionary journey in this book. There are seven concentric circles, three of which are gray. The four circles in black are the topics covered in this book. The first four circles are blown out and filled in with symbols corresponding to the chapters and the heading descriptions for the section.

Our journey is organized in four phases, or *octaves*. Each octave will bring you up the spiral and to the next level of understanding, perspectives, and practices.

Here is what each symbol means:

- *Hummingbird facing right.* The masculine principle of the creative force in all life and the masculine aspects of the individual self. This corresponds to the First Octave.

- *Hummingbird facing left.* The feminine principle of the creative force in all life and the feminine aspects of the individual self. This denotes the Second Octave.

- *Hummingbird pair.* The masculine and feminine principles come together, and the realization that others are a reflection of the self and finding a balance between these principles within the self. The pair of hummingbirds indicates the Third Octave.

- *Hummingbird pair with scarab overhead.* The scarab represents the connection of the left and right hemispheres of the brain. (In chapter 3, we will explore the theory of the physical brain evolutions that underpin the expansions we discuss in this book.) This is the coming together of the heart, emotions, body, and mind in a balanced way. In chapter 7 this opens the door to your True Self or True Essence, which is the part of yourself that is beyond illusion—your fundamental nature. This image represents the Fourth Octave of our explorations.

At the beginning of each octave, a map will orient you to where we are in our journey. An evolution of the hummingbird images appears at the beginning of each chapter. "Expansion Practices" sections include additional information to help you track your progress and keep you motivated. They include guidance on what you may notice in your life as you successfully grow through each step of the process. This will aid you in being aware of why things are shifting as they are, noticing signs that the process is working, and inspiring you to keep going.

I am excited to share this journey with you. My deepest wish is for everyone reading to find their highest path toward self-integration and to claim full creatorship of their reality.

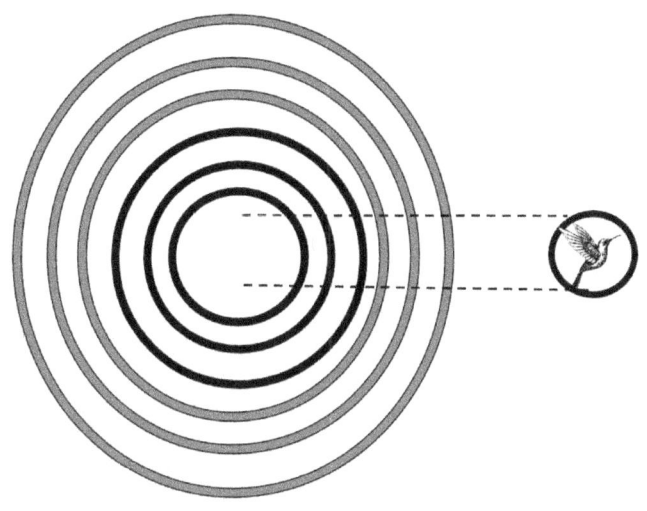

# First Octave:
# Chapters 1 and 2

### The Body Is the Only Technology You Need
### (Physical Plane)

You are not limited to an unconscious experience of your reality. When you only perceive yourself as separate, you navigate your circumstances via reactions fed by old patterns and programming.

**Old Perspective:** *An unconscious directive of "My body is working against me."*

**New Perspective:** *A conscious engagement in "My body is an amazing technology of sensing and experience."*

CHAPTER 1:

# Building Perspective:
# The Evolution of Love and Behavior

*We can only know where we are going if
we know where we have been.*

—Maya Angelou

We start with love defined as a primitive adaptation of the mammalian hormone system that drives behavior for procreation, child-rearing, and group cooperation.

In this chapter, we will discuss this book's more science-heavy aspects. It's essential to start rooted in the perspective of human evolution as we currently understand it. In some respects, this also reflects where general consciousness is within evolution. This acts as the scientific groundwork from which we will "take off" into more uncharted territories and examine less widely accepted ideas, including an expansive exploration of where humanity is headed on the planet at large.

We will start as close to the beginning as science allows us to reach regarding the human experience of love. Traveling to a primitive time when man began to evolve from more animalistic interactions to the affection and bonding we now associate with love. This leads to the development of the family unit, parents, and their children.

We will also track the development of hormones like oxytocin, testosterone, and estrogen through evolutionary behavioral biology. This relatively young branch of science has only begun to unravel the complex drivers of the endocrine system and hormone evolution as a whole.

Although this chapter focuses on science, it will not be a science-heavy discourse. Instead, it will be an evolutionary perspective describing how millions of years have shaped our understanding and experience of love.

Let's begin with the love hormone, oxytocin.

## The Evolutionary Origins of Oxytocin

The hormone oxytocin drives the initial basis of human love—the love bond between mother and offspring that occurs in humans and other mammals.

The ubiquitous nature of attachment love suggests it may be the first type of love, potentially from which all others evolved. The first evidence of this appears approximately 200 million years ago in the Triassic period. This is when dinosaurs roamed the earth, and natural selection favored animals caring for each other to improve survival potential.

When it comes to primitive animals, such as lizards, a mother will abandon her eggs and leave the hatchlings to survive on their own. In fact, if the mother happens to meet her offspring in the future, she's likely to eat them! Knowing this instinctively, the offspring will even flee from her.

*In other words, the "lizard brain" is wired for separation as a strategy for survival.*

The first evolution of love was for the mother to evolve from seeing her offspring as prey to seeing them as something to protect. In turn, this care instilled a sense of safety, leading to trust in the offspring.

An interesting example occurred in the *Morganucodon,* an animal that existed during the transition between reptile and mammal. It is believed to have looked similar to a mouse. The significance of this creature is that it showed mammal-type tooth replacement. Baby *Morganucodons* went from having no teeth to having temporary milk teeth, which they would finally lose to grow adult teeth.

This pattern indicates that *Morganucodons* likely nursed their young, and that's where the hormones come in. It is well known that both the mother and their offspring secrete oxytocin during breastfeeding. When babies nurse, they need more care, which creates an emotional feedback loop as the young depend on the mother as their primary food source.

This is likely why mammals stopped seeing each other solely in terms of danger and food. Further, this shift began more multifaceted relationships between individuals and groups. As bonding continued to develop in mammals, grooming, playing, helping, protecting, and teaching behaviors did as well. This all can be extended to early human behavior, as we, too, are a part of the animal kingdom.

Romantic love between a bonded pair is a relatively recent development, evolutionarily speaking, and is related to the further evolution of oxytocin within the endocrine system. Current accepted theory associates this change with the increased need for help when rearing children.

Parental care is adaptive and has paved the way for other supportive relationships among animals and humans. This level of evolution lays the foundation for societal creation within a species. In most animals, this leads to constructive groups of cooperation for the betterment of the whole. Humans are likely the dominant animal on the planet in part due to this factor.

## Evolution of Hormonal Purpose: Testosterone and Estradiol

It may be surprising that less than 5 percent of mammals engage in long-term exclusive relationships. Let's consider the article "Intimate Relationships Then and Now: How Our Old Psychology Influences Modern Hormonal Processes." This publication explores how our newer psychological adaptations may have rerouted older evolutionary hormonal processes leading to long-term relationships in humans. The authors focused on testosterone and estradiol for their observations on the mate-seeking and mate-competition processes from previous evolutions. They uncover evolutionary connections to multiple behaviors in humans.

In the following section, we will explore the points laid out in this paper to see examples of how evolutionary mechanisms are at the basis of our behaviors.

Testosterone is a hormone that is part of an old evolutionary process that drove the importance of behaviors like social dominance and cooperation. Take our closest relative, the chimpanzee. The chimpanzee mating strategy relies exclusively on dominance and aggression. On the other hand, Bonobos are another close relative but rely more on social cooperation, like grooming, to acquire mates. Surprisingly, this cooperative behavior is coupled with a modest increase in testosterone.

Humans tend to exhibit a more cooperative strategy similar to the bonobos, and like the bonobos, increases in human testosterone are associated with collaboration rather than aggressive behavior. Studies support the idea that a more cooperative and social association strategy is more likely to attract mates.

For example, one study found that in mate-competition circumstances, men with increased testosterone smiled more and made more eye contact with women in comparison to men with lower testosterone levels. Another study by Slatcher et al. showed that women reportedly connected better with men who had higher levels of testosterone.

However, it has also been shown that high testosterone in a mate-competitive situation is associated with dominant behavior. It is important to note that while humans have this tendency, it is not the same as the extreme aggression seen in chimpanzees. While the most successful are the most aggressive in both situations, humans primarily exhibit consensual mating practices, having evolved beyond aggressive strategies to obtain mates.

Of course, we also must consider the complexity of the association between physiology and behavior; examining a psychological adaptation that lead us to a better understanding. As mentioned previously, romantic commitment is a relatively new occurrence. This may be correlated with the development of more advanced brain centers, as humans are the only species able to reflect and communicate a level of obligation within a relationship.

> *The concept of commitment, which necessitates future-oriented thinking, represents a new cognitive adaptation. We are the only species that can predict the consequences of current decisions in the future.*

Sure, other species can predict consequences based on experiences in the past, but these predictions require an immediate circumstance rather than extrapolations of the future. The ability to predict occurs in a human's prefrontal cortex and temporal medial lobes, which are the most recent additions to the brain. These areas are significantly more complex than those found in other primates. The most interesting outcome of romantic commitment and the human brain's evolution is their association with lower testosterone levels in men.

This is potentially because higher testosterone is correlated with more aggressive thoughts and behaviors in many contexts, which is not conducive to a long romantic relationship. Lowered testosterone may also reduce interest in other partners. Furthermore, women in committed relationships have also been found to have lower testosterone levels.

*Lowered testosterone has also been associated with higher involvement in parenting.*

This is often referred to as the trade-off between mating effort and parenting effort. Parenthood presents a need to conserve resources for either that or pair-bonding efforts. Therefore, lowered testosterone levels in committed couples with children may be an evolutionary adaptation to maintain a stable family structure.

With regard to behavior-hormone correlations, estradiol is the most influential form of estrogen found in humans and other mammals. In female primates, estrogen has been correlated with dominance behaviors, such as assertive body postures and physical attacks—in other words, behaviors generally associated with men with higher testosterone levels.

However, it is interesting to note that testosterone can be easily converted to estrogen in males, females, and in all mammals. This evolution likely allows for quick changes in physiological response to external circumstances. For example, child-rearing necessitates a different approach than defense from a potential threat.

While the full role of estradiol is not entirely understood, there are a few interesting observations. In a study by de Catanzaro et al., male mice housed next to female mice had an increase in urinary estradiol levels over multiple days. Furthermore, according to observations by Antonio et al., male rats treated with estradiol exhibited increased sexual receptivity to females.

When estrogen receptors have been repressed in male mice, they are incapable of engaging in sexual investigation. If there is no interest or drive to check out females, then no procreation will occur. We often think of estrogen as a female hormone, but in reality, both sexes need it to have an interest in reproduction and the most primitive systems that drive love.

Evolutionarily, human women's sexual behaviors can be linked to estrogen when the chance for reproduction is greatest. Estrogen increases during ovulation and acts to motivate conception behaviorally. Furthermore, single women and those experiencing their monthly cycle tend to have higher estrogen levels, which supports competition for mates. Therefore, estradiol is an essential contributor to sexual behavior, motivation, and increased receptivity, particularly in women. Estrogen is also linked to increased experiences of social bonding, such as nurturing and intimacy, in both sexes.

It's been observed that nurturing behavior activates estrogen receptors in rats, which creates a situation where maternal behavior results in a desire to engage in more maternal behavior. Interestingly, the same holds for male mice. When treated with estradiol, male mice exhibited increased paternal behavior. In humans, this type of interaction has mainly been studied in terms of care for children but also has an application in pair-bonded relationships.

While estradiol levels for women are typically correlated with mate competition and sexual-drive behaviors, this new psychological adaptation supports its role in creating intimacy and social connections. This brings us to the idea of attachment in romantic relationships. Attachment theory was initially established to describe the infant-caregiver dynamic but can also be applied to human adult romantic attachment.

## Attachment Theory:
## An Evolution of the Romantic Bond

John Bowlby conceptualized attachment theory in the 1950s. He proposed that the original infant-caregiver attachment behavioral system may have been adapted by natural selection to bond adult romantic partners to one another.

This means that the same physiological system that evolved for bonding between mother and offspring also bonds partners. Romantic attachment theory emphasizes the importance of the individual's experience of their unique human-caregiver bond, as it creates a template for future close relationships. Attachment behavior has three main types: avoidant, anxious, and secure.

Avoidantly and anxiously attached children learned that their needs could not be met by their caregivers, so they adopted psychological strategies to cope. Avoidantly attached children exhibit uncomfortableness when partners or even friends want to get closer. While anxiously attached children tend to worry and be concerned that they are not getting the support or love they need. Many of these behaviors are unconsciously driven.

Lastly, securely attached individuals report low levels of avoidant and anxious behavior and have little issue meeting their needs and becoming closer to others. Attachment behaviors can drive our individual experience of love based on patterns that arise from early parental dynamics. This is important to note because attachment tendencies can often become subconscious drivers of behavior and likely are related to our hormones.

The correlation between attachment behaviors and hormones has yet to be completely understood, though some specific patterns have been observed. For example, one study showed that men and women with higher levels of estradiol had a more secure attachment bond, and this was especially true when there was a desire for closeness. Secure bonding may refocus the estradiol away from dominant or competitive behaviors toward nurturant and intimate behaviors.

However, when women have weaker attachment bonds with men, they may show inhibition toward physical intimacy during ovulation (when there is the greatest chance for conception). There may also be other hormones at play, given the complex endocrine dance that drives this behavior.

# Evolution

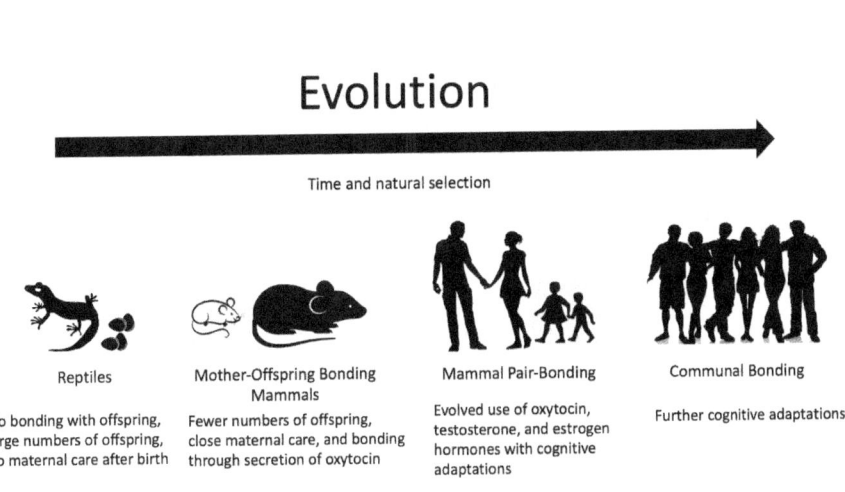

Time and natural selection

**Reptiles**
No bonding with offspring, large numbers of offspring, no maternal care after birth

**Mother-Offspring Bonding Mammals**
Fewer numbers of offspring, close maternal care, and bonding through secretion of oxytocin

**Mammal Pair-Bonding**
Evolved use of oxytocin, testosterone, and estrogen hormones with cognitive adaptations

**Communal Bonding**
Further cognitive adaptations

As mentioned, hormonal evolution has shifted from separate, more animal-like interactions to familial groups and eventually community organization. This evolution supports the survival of our species.

Our animal evolution has been one that favors connection, bonding, and love.

The early stages of what we call love today likely arose due to the development of oxytocin, initially starting between mother and offspring during childbirth and nursing, but now we also know that it is secreted during sex and even exercise.

This bonds couples and individuals together with their communities. Oxytocin secretion also occurs when we feel empathy for a stranger and in low-intensity touches from others or even ourselves. Such behavior has become a potential self-soothing practice. In chapter 3, we will explore the felt experiences associated with key hormones and examine the purpose of those hormones in health.

The following section moves more into "boundary science," pushing our understanding of our natural world and the more energetic perspectives of our reality. As we move in this direction, we will consider how the theory of metamorphic fields correlates with evolution, as they pertain to the microcosms of our experience all the way down to the cellular level and up to the macrocosm of the universe at the largest scales.

## An Introduction to Metamorphic Fields

Metamorphic fields were first hypothesized in 1910 by Alexander G. Gurwitsch and aided by experimental work from Ross Granville Harrison. Gurwitsch deduced that there were unseen fields that drove physical development in utero. Dr. Rupert Sheldrake, a contemporary in the field, has made efforts to bring this science to the public with his seventeen books. His most recent is *Ways to Go Beyond: Seven Spiritual Practices in the Scientific Age*.

At its most basic level, Dr. Sheldrake sees metamorphic fields as the memory of nature itself. He views the laws of nature as habits that have accrued over time, the experiences of the animal and plant world, and evolution itself. However, evolution, as Sheldrake talks about, is not just about the genes that are passed on. It is an intelligent field that organizes form to create.

In biology, genes are seen as the masters of creation. However, this raises a question: If we share so many genes with other animals, how do we have such diversity in living beings? For example, we share 98.8 percent of our DNA with chimpanzees, 90 percent with cats, and 80 percent with cows. Genes and the products they make are not sufficient to understand how decisions are made in the complex development of living things. Metamorphic fields are the missing link that governs this level.

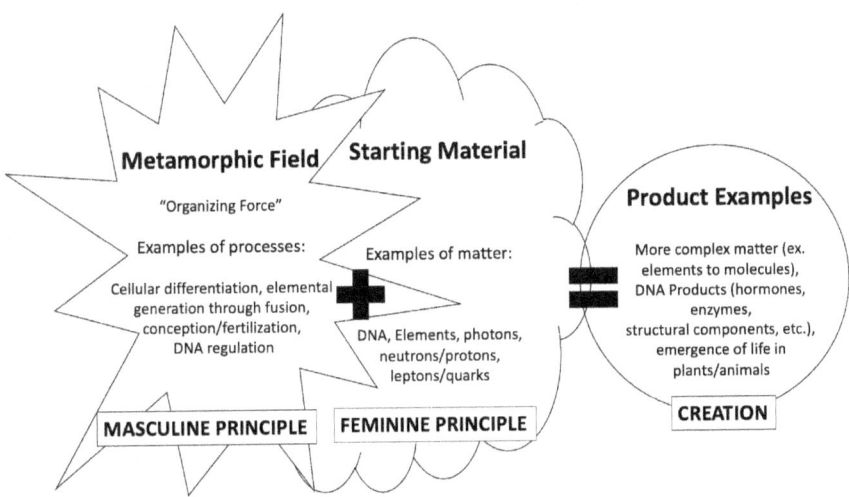

In general, metamorphic fields are the unseen forces that impose a pattern of organization on otherwise random matter (ex. genes, fundamental particles, electrons). This is a foundational concept to remember as we move through our journey, as it applies to many other areas of creation. In our current discussion, we are getting our first glimpse of polarity. The masculine principle (a force) working with the feminine principle (starting materials) is the polarity of creation in our reality.

There is an important relationship between metamorphic fields and evolution. These fields work to perfect creation at all levels. There is a global field and fields down to the DNA of different species of plants and animals. Each one of these fields has a frequency. The slower the frequency, the slower the evolution. While the faster the frequency, the faster the evolution. The Earth, for example, has a slow frequency, and evolutions occur over millions of years.

Sheldrake suggests that our most impactful fields are inherited through genetic lineage within the same species. He terms this *nonlocal resonance*, which conveys an "instinctive" memory. In Sheldrake's book *Presence of the Past*, he mentions, "The more similar the organism is to previous organisms, the greater the influence of morphic resonance." He further points out that the more organisms that have come before, the more impact they will have on future generations.

However, metamorphic fields can also affect behavior collectively. Patterns of behavior have been observed to spread very quickly through a species. The first level in which this occurs is heredity.

William McDougal researched how learning was transferred through generations of a species. Beginning in 1920 and spanning thirty years, he trained rats to escape a specially designed water maze. There were two exits, one that was illuminated, and would deliver a slight shock when the rat would pass through. The second exit was completely safe to leave.

It took the first generation of rats about 165 trials to learn to take the dim exit consistently. The next generation of rats learned much quicker, and by the thirteenth litter, the rats only made about twenty errors. McDougall even corrected for intelligence. When he selected the least intelligent rats to breed for the next round, they still showed a significant increase in learning from the previous generation.

Ancestral themes often come up in sessions I have with clients. Our ancestors send us understandings, tendencies, and sometimes even beliefs that served them in their lives. These are passed down for us to utilize and build on to evolve. It invites the question, What will your life experience and growth contribute to your lineage?

When patterns arise from the ancestorial lineage in my sessions with clients, there is a "stuckness" to the energy, signaling a change of some sort is needed. This occurs most often when it is at the level of the belief system. While those who came before have many gifts to bestow, sometimes the patterns limit us, and the energy could be redirected to create more freedom in the client's current life.

The client is freed from its constraints by pinpointing the limiting belief passed down and assisting its evolution. These come up in sessions when the client is either ready to evolve past a certain point or when the greater collective is working to evolve beyond certain themes. The work I describe here is similar to ThetaHealing, which Vianna Stibal developed.

What are beliefs really? An individual's brain looks for patterns and emotional prompts that flag an important learning experience. Then, the belief is invested in, and the brain is primed to search for additional supporting evidence to reinforce it. This is an adaptive action of the human brain, aiding us in understanding how to navigate the world via day-to-day learning. It's survival.

However, beliefs impede us when they are limiting in some way. This is because beliefs are based on perspectives and not truths. One can become very intolerant of other views, and internal or external conflict can result. Intolerant beliefs have been the seed of many wars.

For example, if you believe that the God of your religion is the true God and all others are a false God, then you risk making everyone outside of your religion an enemy.

Beliefs can also be passed down from our ancestors as unfinished business from their lifetimes. You can work on these beliefs one by one as you become aware. However, one of the opportunities this book offers is to pull yourself out of being driven solely by old patterns from metamorphic fields and consciously work *with* them to create your experience.

The difference between the two is being unconsciously driven by past influences or realizing the patterns were passed down and repurposing them. It is the beginning of becoming a creator with the powerful metamorphic field.

One example could be the influence of marriage from a previous generation who saw marriage as transactional and based on how the partnership improved financial stability for one family. You may have found this pattern repeated in romantic relationships, as they seem transactional. This is when you want a different type of marriage based on connection, love, and partnership. You can consciously repurpose the pattern passed down and focus that energy on other types of partnerships in your life (for example, business partnerships).

Then, you are creating the stability your ancestors craved in their experience but could not complete. You don't necessarily need to heal the pattern but repurpose it to meet the need. Not all patterns passed down necessarily create blocks for you, but many can.

We have seen how metamorphic fields affect the generation of the physical world as well as consciousness. You may be scratching your head and wondering how this relates to love. What is important here is to learn the basic mechanisms of our current experience of love:

the evolution of hormones and behavior and the unseen fields that guide all evolution—metamorphic fields.

In the next section, we will approach another foundational block in our exploration of love. Context is everything! Knowing how our human love hardware developed on a more subtle, energetic level lets us know what we are working with and gives us clues on how to continue to develop it.

## Layers of the Auric Field

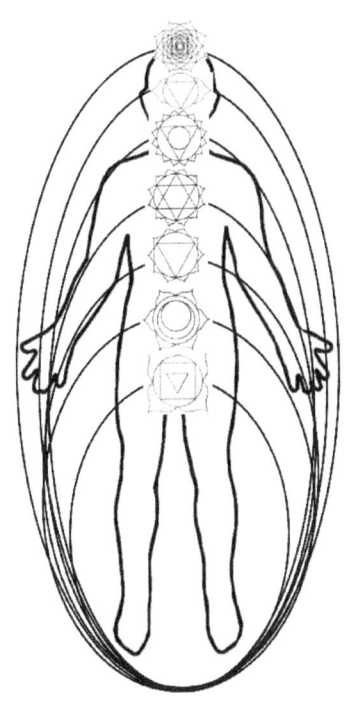

| SPIRITUAL PLANE (Spirit Body) |
| :--- |
| Mental Spirit: Crown Chakra 7 |
| Emotional Spirit: Third Eye Chakra 6 |
| Body Spirit: Throat Chakra 5 |
| **ASTRAL PLANE (Soul Body)** |
| Astral Body: Heart Chakra 4 |
| **PHYSICAL PLANE (Physical Body)** |
| Mental Body: Solar Plexus Chakra 3 |
| Emotional Body: Sacral Chakra 2 |
| Physical Body: Root Chakra 1 |

## The Chakra System

According to the teachings of Dr. Sri Amit Ray, there are 114 chakras. While we will focus on what are considered the primary seven, know that many other centers are feeding energy in, through, and out of your body. While other chakras are referred to as minor or even micro chakras, each is important to the whole. This is the system that the technology of the body is constantly using to engage with your environment.

The seven chakras each project out from the body and create layers of an egg-shaped field that comprises your aura. The image above has been simplified to some degree to show that the chakras all feed your field. The shape of your magnetic energy field is a torus. This geometry is like a thick donut with you in the center. The magnetic field runs along the surface of the torus and inside to the center of the donut shape.

This book will first focus on balancing each aspect of the Physical Plane to attain more profound balance and access to the Astral Plane. I see the Astral Plane as currently having three sections: outer heart, main heart, and higher heart. The heart has multiple levels because it bridges the first three chakras (root, sacral, and solar plexus) and the expanded chakras (throat, third eye, and crown). This mirrors the human as the bridge, or heart, between the Earth and Spirit.

The first three chakras mainly concern your human experience before they are unlocked and opened. You will go through this process to release the density acquired in these chakras and take responsibility for what you create in your life. After the chakras are opened, there will be more access for the expanded energies of your spirit to begin to flow differently.

Our journey aims to give you access to more of your spiritual being-ness and your True Self. This is the beginning of integrating your current human existence with your eternal self. It is a recollection of who you are beyond this incarnation and is a birth to the more spiritual aspects of self.

After this, you may not need further guidance on your path as you learn and experience that you have everything you need inside of you. After the heart is activated, you can see that the path leads to the expanded chakras, going back through the themes of mind, emotions, and body but at a more spiritual level. The remembering continues.

Our exploration of these energy centers begins with the root chakra and how the themes of this chakra relate to the discussion in this chapter. Each chakra has a specific way of moving energy to create your existence. In truth, each one is related to themes like potential, Love, and polarity, but in different facets. We will examine some of these facets and how they relate to your evolution.

## Root Chakra (Including the Knee and Foot Chakras): I AM Potential

There is a relationship between Love and each chakra. As we will find throughout this book, Love is a permeating force throughout all creation. Opening the first four chakras aims to upgrade humans' access to Love.

The root chakra is our first energy center located at the spine's base. It is associated with a red color frequency, masculine polarity, and fire element. We will also consider the minor chakras of each foot and each knee, as their themes feed directly to the root chakra. Their inclusion is important because we need to activate awareness in our legs to activate the body completely.

I have found that when only the seven main chakras are focused on, there is an incompleteness of flow and awareness in the body. Further, the themes of the foot and knee chakras are also where there are strong influences from the metamorphic field of ancestry.

Much of the information presented in the chakra sections of this book comes from Matías de Stephano's "Universe Within" class. I have found his perspectives go beyond the basic information currently available about many things, especially the chakras.

To begin, the foot chakras are your human connection to the ground. They represent your destiny and where you have been and are going. This also includes a strong component of where your lineage has been and the influences of tradition—the paths others have walked before us. De Stephano points out that much of your personality and drives have been built by the difficulties of your ancestors.

This means that drives from ancestry are not the truth of who you are. Therefore, while still connected to ancestry, the information in your feet determines the basic patterns of some situations you continue to create in your life.

At any time, you can take control of your life's purpose to serve what you want to create and not be controlled by your ancestors' unfinished business. You can do this by creating a balance between what you think (spirit), feel (soul), and do (body). Throughout our journey, you will aim to align these exact areas of yourself: thoughts, feelings, and actions.

Next, we move up to the knee chakras. The right side of the body is related to the masculine, and the left is associated with the feminine. These two columns of polarity hold you between heaven and Earth. The right knee chakra corresponds to the Tree of Wisdom, and the left is related to the Tree of Life.

The Tree of Life corresponds to the metamorphic field and the aspects of our physical evolution. This includes the information from all life that ever existed on this planet. Evolutions here are reflections between the food our ancestors consumed to stimulate activations, the food you consume, and your relationship to your body. This is why it is crucial to cultivate deeper acquaintance with your body and an intuition of what nourishment it needs.

This design is encoded in DNA as the four amino acid base pairs: adenine, cytosine, guanine, and thymine. These are the main elements of creation that hold all the information to create form. DNA is actually Kundalini and holds all your potential within each cell of the body. The potential needs activation to transcend the normal human experience to include your more spiritual aspects of the divine within.

*Kundalini* is a Sanskrit word meaning "coiled." This is cosmic energy in its potential form in every cell but lies dormant until the root chakra is activated, which can be coerced, nurtured, or allowed. When forced, activation can cause many difficult symptoms, including extreme fatigue, uncomfortable electrical pulses in the body, pain, digestive dysfunction, and heart palpitations, among others.

Throughout your journey through this book, you may feel your Kundalini awakening. When that opening is nurtured with meditation, increased presence and awareness, and consistent practice of exercises like alternate nostril breathing (see chapter 2 "Expansion Practices for the Physical Body"), receptiveness and growth can occur, and disruptive symptoms may be minimized.

Sometimes, an event will cause a spontaneous Kundalini awakening, such as an accident or near-death experience. Around the age of forty, the chance of activating this energy heightens. Once awakened, this energy moves through the chakras, helps to activate them, and provides fodder for a deeper connection to your true spiritual nature and all that is.

This is a part of the evolution of our energy bodies. At the same time, not a focus of this book, Kundalini awakening and fostering may be part of the journey you will take. If you want further information, I recommend reading the book *Serpent Rising: The Kundalini Compendium* by Neven Paar.

The Tree of Wisdom side, represented by your right leg, is what gives each creation meaning. De Stephano perceives it as an invisible string that connects all things at the quantum level. This is the smallest level known to physical reality, the realm of electrons and smaller fundamental particles like quarks. String theory then explains that when we go smaller than these fundamental particles, there are just vibrating strings, much like what de Stephano is pointing to. They vibrate at fundamental frequencies of existence, where similar frequencies resonate with the deeper fabric of reality.

The Tree of Wisdom is the level where everything is connected. However, it seems as if everything is separate because, in the third dimension, everything is wrapped in a package of information from the vibratory field of the Tree of Wisdom. In this way, each human is a separate packet of information that creates a specific perspective of reality. One packet equals one piece of the truth. This is why you need others on your path to help you see more aspects of the truth and what reality is.

To access the full information in the Tree of Life and the Tree of Wisdom, you must be aware of yourself at a higher level. To activate the Kundalini of the cells, you can modify what you consume (feminine) or experience light (masculine). For the feminine aspect, it is the food, emotions, and ideas that you consume. For the masculine, evolution on our planet has been driven by light, first with photosynthesis. It continues to be a source of activation, as the sun has frequencies that can modify and change DNA.

These themes of ancestry in both the feet and ankles then feed into the root chakra to create the potential relating to your specific incarnation. The root chakra in Sanskrit means "base" or "support." This is where the information from your ancestors and all past creations moves into your physical and energetic body to create potential energy at the base of your spine. This is the first place within you that Kundalini can be activated and awakened.

Regarding Love, the root chakra is the love and support of your ancestors channeled directly into you. You are their evolution. They have created a strong base for you to continue to create. Commonly seen with parents, your ancestors are projecting their wants for you here. You can hear their messages and decide your own path. Recognize the deep love they send to you to bless your life.

This chakra is also related to sexuality and will open when there is safety around this theme. Safety equals love in this chakra. While sexuality and survival are strong essences here, they represent some of the most common blocks people have in our society. At some point in our history, it was decided that from the navel down was "not good," and the drive toward "good" was above in the spiritual realm.

This perspective disconnected us from the Earth, matter, our bodies, and the fullness of our human experience. The reality is that heaven is already on Earth and within you. Spiritual people often talk about going to the higher dimensions (fourth, fifth, and sixth), but the truth is that they already exist all around you. Awakening to them is what is needed. Spirituality tends to keep heaven separate from Earth, although they are one and the same.

The mind of God makes all matter and is heaven. One of the beautiful paradoxes is that this all exists and also does not exist. From a quantum mechanical view, atoms comprise 99 percent empty space. So you see, when you leave matter, you also leave heaven. Then you see that your job is to balance matter, not to leave it.

In your human incarnation, when you become responsible for the things you have created, you balance and harmonize them. When you Love matter, the polarity of it (light and dark, masculine and feminine), then you can see its purpose and not have any expectations from it. Loving without expectation *is* Unconditional Love.

This is the maturation talked about previously. As mentioned in the description of the knee chakras, we are the intermediary between above (God) and below (Earth). When we are conscious of our creations and bring balance, then the technology of our human body becomes a powerful force of creation in the world, galaxy, universe, and beyond.

> *The Earth itself is conscious, and we are all a reflection of the Earth's state of evolution.*

The energy that feeds the root chakra comes directly from the Earth to the body, and when unblocked, it then travels to the root to God and back. This planet receives its energy directly from the sun and the sun directly from creation. Just as humans are individuals, the Earth is also an individual going through an evolution of consciousness.

The macrocosm and microcosm are often referred to in the phrase *as above, so below*. This saying points to the idea that we are mirrors of different aspects of reality and the universe. This pattern of reality can also be described as a fractal. This correspondence means that interworking of your body mirrors the interworking of the universe.

In geometry, a fractal pattern is something that is repeated at different size scales. For example, you will see self-similarity in the structure of leaves. The large veins you see across a leaf are mirrored in smaller patterns between those veins. Nature is full of this! Romanesco vegetables, trees, coastlines, and even galaxies are fractal.

There are many other examples of this, as microcosms (smaller environments) often reflect the macrocosms (larger environments) and vice versa. This represents the beautiful balance and reflection of the universe at every level first postulated by ancient philosophers like

Plato, pointing to the possibility that the universe itself is a living system in a constant state of interacting and responding.

You can apply this idea to literally anything. However, in terms of the root chakra, this means that you are a direct reflection of the Earth (feminine character), her consciousness, God (masculine character), and his consciousness. In the root chakra, these are the twin flames of polarity and the first ingredient of creation.

This is spirit, and it is everywhere. It becomes matter through the energy produced by the soul (emotions). This is seen in all creation, from procreation between two people to activations in yourself. In your human experience, spirit needs to feel and express itself in matter. To connect with this, you need to become more in tune with your body.

This is exactly where humanity has been stuck for many thousands of years. We have acquired shame about our bodies, and this has blocked our evolution. The truth is that the root chakra, your sexual organs, and the hypothalamus can create primordial energy from divinity in every cell of your body.

This is not about sex with another person or yourself. This is the energy of Kundalini, your reconnection to the divine. Tantra is an ancient way to manage this energy, but first you must become aware and open to its existence.

To have access to your root chakra energies, you have to bring awareness to and release the stuck energy within this chakra. In the "Expanding Exercises" chapter, the humming meditation practice will help with this. But first, you also need to build a relationship with your body.

When you touch your arm and give yourself a massage, it releases oxytocin and connects you more deeply to yourself. Practice this and see what emotions come up. Do you feel uncomfortable in some way? Is there shame coming up? This is an opportunity to bring your awareness to these issues. By releasing oxytocin and an internal monologue of safety and reassurance, you can begin to open these previously stuck places.

The root chakra can easily be blocked from birth due to the influences of ancestry, survival instincts, and all that is primal. At the human level, it also includes the activation of the fight-or-flight response, which links to the most primitive part of our brain. Each chakra contains energy that both projects out from the body and receives energy from the universe. Creating safety for the body is a priority when unblocking the root chakra.

> *When consciousness evolves to open and inhabit a chakra fully, it allows you to take conscious involvement in the themes that activate the chakras rather than unconsciously reflecting your density (stuck emotions) back to you. Using consciousness to do this is part of an individual spiritual maturation process.*

When you take responsibility for what you create in this world and acknowledge your spiritual nature, new dimensions of expansion and creation open to you. This permeates every facet of life and manifests differently in individuals based on their experience and personality.

Beyond the individual, the collective has much density with similar themes that must be cleared. When you clear your own density with conscious awareness, you are helping to clear it for all humans. Remember, the microcosm affects the macrocosm and vice versa.

Explore the expansion practices in the next chapter to integrate and apply these perspectives and energies of your root chakra.

# Chapter Recap

## Illuminated Takeaway

*We have evolved hormones that drive specific basic human behaviors. These are governed by a field of intelligence called metamorphic fields, which drive human evolution with or without the individual's participation.*

In this chapter, we laid the foundational understanding that one purpose of human experience is purely evolution. Of course, you don't need this book to experience evolution. You already have simply by existing because you were your parents' evolution the moment you were born—and you have certainly had many other evolutions in your life.

Next acknowledging the dual nature of all that comprises the whole: the above (spirit) and the below (human). Understanding this is the first step in opening your consciousness to further evolution. Evolution then becomes the relationship between consciousness, spirit, and the human, which requires purification of the densities we have acquired so that we can live from our more genuine nature.

**At this point in your journey, you may begin to experience . . .**

- New perspectives that create awareness of the purpose of hormones as they relate to human behavioral evolution.
- A curiosity about metamorphic fields and the implications of this unseen organizing intelligence.
- A spark of interest in understanding the relationship between the energy body and chakras to the material in this chapter and your journey.

CHAPTER 2:

# Expansion Practices for the Physical Body

I n your first month's practices, you lay the practical groundwork for increasing flexibility in the "doing" and "being" aspects of your human experience, paving a road for the maturation of the self. After practicing for some time, you may begin to have more access to the present moment.

You will notice old, automatic behaviors and realize you have a choice. What will you do with a renewed sense of choice? You will find that releasing old habits brings in the ability to see opportunities that before went unseen! An increased ability to perceive and connect with the Love already around you is opening.

The practices in this chapter will help you develop a connection with:

- New perspectives to create awareness and flexibility in your actions
- Examples of what it means to have an understanding of higher frequency emotions and how they affect your life

- Increased feelings of calm and presence as you commit to a daily breathwork and meditation practice.

Before continuing to the next chapter, take four weeks to practice the meditations, journaling, and other exercises.

This marks the beginning of an evolution of your individual experience. These practices are designed to help build awareness, strengthen personal embodiment, and provide an expanded understanding of your reality. Building these practices gives you more access to increased states of ease, joy, and fulfillment in your life. In addition to meditation and journaling, the first chapter of practices will start with two simple additional exercises to establish structures that can rewire your human experience.

Check-in on your progress with your diet at this point. Do you need more support to understand better what your body needs for nutrition? If so, consider reaching out to an Ayurvedic practitioner. Creating mastery over the physical body opens the opportunity for further expansion and will act as the basis of your journey.

Take your time with the expanded practices. If you feel the urge to skip steps, remember that your mind wants to hurry through something that cannot be rushed. You are creating new neurological connections and working on your energetic system. Be patient with yourself and the process.

## Practice Overview and Checklist

### Meditation

- Follow the instructions in the "Building Your Meditation" section.

## Daily Journal

- Check in with your experiences. Note any recent mental or emotional contractions, expansions, or questions you may reflect on.
- How have you been finding the new practices? What has been difficult or easy?
- Reflect on any new experiences you have during these exercises.
- As detailed below, write about an experience with the Steps to Change a Pattern exercise.
- What is your current relationship with movement? How might you like this to change?
- Check in with your diet. Consider whether there are any changes you would like to commit to over the next four weeks.
- Moment of expansion: What is your current relationship with being on autopilot and experiencing presence? As you notice these different states occurring during your day, consider how each makes you feel.

## Tools to Practice

This section will track the growing number of tools you have at your disposal during meditations and in situations in everyday life. This helps hardwire the changes. Your beginning practices are:

- Meditation*
- Journaling*
- Watching the Thinker*
- Steps to Change a Pattern*
- Movement*

*New practice

# Building Your Meditations

You will create a meditation practice to get the most out of your journey and this book. Even if you have an established meditation method, please use the following, as it is specific to the explorations laid out in this book.

In this section, we will assemble the essential elements for daily meditations. This meditation amalgamates teachings from many sources, and is strongly influenced by Matías de Stephano's meditation introduced in his "Universe Within" class. Additional practices suggested in this book can be added after meditation as a further exploration or throughout your day.

It is best to meditate first thing in the morning when you wake up. If time is tight in the morning, dedicate fifteen minutes. If you have more time and are interested in sitting in meditation, then do so.

Meditation aims to access both sides of your brain and integrate information into and through your body's cells, which creates activations. Your auric field brings information about every level of your reality to your chakras. By meditating, this information can be brought in and assimilated.

The main components of all your meditation practices will be:

1. Readying yourself and your space
2. Creating safety and comfort
3. Breathwork
4. Humming to open the body
5. Meditation
6. Closing your practice

Making a voice recording to guide yourself during meditations may be helpful until they become a habit. You will have two breathwork methods during your meditation. Please do both, as they each have a different purpose.

Let's get started.

## Readying Yourself and Your Space

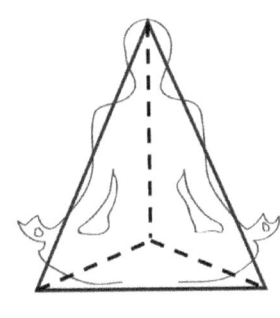

This is a daily ceremony you will engage in. Have a dedicated space for meditation, a sacred space you can come to every day where you won't be disturbed. You can keep it simple or elaborate (candles, incense, essential oils, crystals, special pillows, etc.). Whatever you create, do so with intention. Ensure everything has a purpose. Of course, if you are traveling, you can meditate anywhere. Having a consistent space to come back to daily can aid in creating safety and deepening your practice.

Now that your space is set up sit comfortably in a cross-legged position with your eyes closed throughout your meditation. You want to create a tetrahedral shape with your body by leaning your back slightly forward so that your head is the top point on the tetrahedron. The tetrahedron is the first shape of matter; it repeats itself into many fractal structures to become everything. Through it, you are connecting with the unit structure of the universe.

However, if that is uncomfortable, sit in a chair with your feet on the ground and your back straight. Close your eyes to signal to your body that your awareness is shifting from the outside to the inside.

Follow these steps to begin your practice:

1. Remain in a tetrahedral position (preferred) throughout your meditation or in a chair with eyes closed and a straight back.

2.  Next, bring *gentle* movement to the joints of your body. Do each movement five to eight times. Stay present in the body and feel the stretches as they occur. Start making small circles with your lower torso, then reverse the direction. Now move your spine in each of the four directions, first to the right, to open up the side body. Hold in the stretch for a few seconds, then repeat with the left side. Now lean forward, leading with your chest as you try to touch your two shoulder blades together. Now, move backward, creating a curve in your back; your head can drop forward slightly to stretch the neck gently.

3.  Then, bring your arms out to your sides and feel that stretch. Now, bring them up above your head and stretch. Next, bring gentle movement to your neck. Move your neck by looking right (hold for a few seconds), then look left (hold for a few seconds). Repeat on each side. Continue to bring movement to your neck by moving your right ear toward your right shoulder, then hold for a few seconds. Repeat on the left side. Now, look up at the ceiling, move your neck backward, and hold for five seconds. Then open and close your jaw a few times. Repeat any of the movements you are drawn to.

4.  Now roll your wrists, make a fist, then extend your fingers. Roll your ankles and contract and extend your toes. Then, sense whether there is any other way your body would like to move and move in that way, with the intention of opening up the joints and energy flow within the body. Finish with an exhale to release any extra energy you liberated.

If you have any pain or physical issues with movement, please consult your doctor before doing these movements. None of these movements should be harsh, and there should be no pain. They should feel like a gentle stretch.

Next, move on to a physical touch exercise that will help pull you into your body, create safety, and begin to open up the hormonal system.

## Creating Safety and Comfort

Now that the nervous system is calm and receptive, we will bring awareness throughout your body with a physical touch scan. This opens the hormonal system to release oxytocin and other hormones, brings you into your body, and declares safety that will allow more significant openings within your chakras. Anytime during this process, exhale through your mouth to release any energy that may build up.

1. Tell your body you are closing your eyes and going inside, bringing the body along with you. Every time you reach a new place, take a deep breath and exhale to release any energy. Start by connecting your hands with your feet. Use a firm and friendly touch as you bring your awareness first to your toes and then to the bottoms of your feet. Use this time to connect with and inhabit your body more deeply. Now move from the tops of your feet to your ankles.

2. Continue up your calves, sending intentions of safety and your awareness to the front and back of your lower legs. Tell your body that you are doing this meditation for its greatest good. Then, move to your knees. With your hands on your knees, feel yourself deepening into your body.

3. Next, move up to your thighs, feeling the strength in the physicality. Treat your body with a sense of love. Connect energetically and with soft intention using a firm touch, bringing awareness and safety. Then, move up to your hips with appreciation. Send warmth with intention to this area.

4. Now, move up to your belly and lower back. Feel the safety and reassurance you are bringing to fill up this area. Then

move to your stomach and chest, spending as much time as feels good to bring in comfort and loving support to this area.

5. Continue down your arms, inviting a sense of security and safety, almost like you are hugging yourself. Then, move up your neck and to the back of your head.

6. Next is your face. Give yourself a gentle massage, sending love and safety to the different areas of your face. Last, we move to the top of the head and scalp. Use your fingertips to comfortably massage your scalp, anchoring your awareness.

7. Take one last deep breath through your nose and exhale through the mouth to release any freed energy.

The next step in your daily meditation is at least five to seven minutes of breathwork.

## Breathwork

*To learn how to breathe is to become spiritual*

—Matías de Stephano

### Alternate Nostril Breathing (ANB)

Start with ANB as your daily go-to for meditation or anytime you seek a more centered, calm state throughout your day.

While you only need two to three minutes of this practice to bring you to a more balanced state, you are encouraged to do more when you have time. Start the day with this practice for a clearer mind. You can make this your primary process to deal with stress, as it reduces anxiety and rejuvenates the nervous system.

ANB has been practiced for thousands of years and is a part of the yogic tradition of pranayama. In Sanskrit, it is called *nadi shodhana pranayama,* which means "subtle energy clearing."

This quick and exceptionally effective practice balances the left and right sides of the brain and body. Each nostril connects to the opposite side of the brain (the right nostril to the left side and vice versa). This practice will help you become more alert and relaxed. It also positively affects blood pressure, heart rate variability, lung function and helps clear toxins from the body. However, do not attempt if you have a congested nose.

It's important to note that any efforts toward balancing your breathing (even simply a slow inhale through the nose and a brief hold followed by a slow exhale) will bring some restoration to your body and mind. Therefore, be conscious of your breathing throughout the day. Pay special attention if you find yourself breathing through your mouth throughout, have sleep apnea, or have been told that you snore.

You can work to remedy this by bringing awareness during the day, taping your mouth closed at night, or even talking to your doctor about getting a sleep apnea device. The importance of your breathing cannot be overstated. If you want more information on this, the book *Breath: The New Science of a Lost Art* by James Nestor is an interesting read.

*The importance of breathwork is that it opens the door to meditation.*

Practice ANB as follows:

1. Re-find your tetrahedral position or in a chair with your eyes closed.
2. Use your right thumb on your right hand to close your right nostril, then exhale entirely through your left nostril.
3. Next, inhale through your left nostril. Then close the left nostril nostril with either your right pinky or ring finger. Both nostrils will be closed for one or two seconds (although you can play with elongating this time).

4. Open the right nostril and exhale through this side.

5. Inhale through the right nostril and then close this nostril.

6. Open the left nostril and exhale through the left side.

Continue this cycle for at least two minutes, and end your practice by exhaling through your left nostril. Afterward, take stock of how you feel. People often feel calmer and more centered, even after just a few rounds of ANB. Continue with box breathing.

### *Box Breathing*

1. You should still be in a tetrahedral position or a chair with closed eyes.

2. While doing box breathing, only breathe through your nose. Inhale for a count of three or four.

3. Next, hold for the same amount of time.

4. Then, release the breath for the same count.

5. Hold again for a count of three or four. That is one round.

6. Continue and try to expand the time to five or six and up to a seven or eight-count maximum. However, if three or four feels most comfortable, stick with that.

7. Continue this way of breathing for about three to five minutes.

Continue to build the practice by bringing sound and vibration into your meditation.

## Humming to Open the Body

You listen to music and play instruments, creating frequency and sound that have therapeutic effects on the body. Remember that frequency and light are the universe's languages, from the smallest fundamental particles to large astronomical bodies like the sun and galaxies. Your voice also has the capacity to create frequency and direct energy.

After your safety creation practice and breathwork, continue building your meditation by adding humming to open your glands and chakras with the following steps:

1. You should still be in a tetrahedral position or a chair with closed eyes. Breathe in and out through your nose during the entire exercise.

2. Experiment with a natural humming sound. Find the tone that feels like your resonant frequency. No trying is necessary. Find that natural, effortless sound that flowers up from your throat. Tune into the healing resonance you are creating and be present with it.

3. Let the sound carry out for one full breath and notice the vibration in your sinuses. Carry that vibration back into your brain and feel it activating and opening the important hypothalamus and pituitary glands there. These glands are now sending signals to ready the chakras to open. Feel and know that your system is being readied to open them.

4. Continuing to hum throughout this practice, pull that energy into the rest of your head. Feel your ears resonate with the sound. Now, it moves down the throat and your neck. You may feel pulsations here or tingles as the energy moves. Continue to bring the vibration down your arms and to your fingertips.

5. Then, move your awareness to your upper torso, bringing the vibration down to the body. Next, take your time as you become aware of your stomach area and the rest of your lower torso, then your hips, down your legs to your knees, and then your lower legs into your feet.

6. Now, the frequency has reached the whole body; feel the vibrations everywhere. All your cells are in resonance. Your body is ready to open the chakras and integrate the available information. Bring the vibration of your hum down to your feet.

## Meditation: Root, Knee, and Foot Chakra

Each "Expansion Practices" section has a humming exercise associated with each additional chakra in your meditation. Daily chakra meditations with sound will help to open and clear the flow between energy centers and integrate information within you. The goal is to promote more profound cellular activations throughout your body with this information. You can play with doing this part of the meditation with or without humming. Maybe other sounds, words, or songs come through. Follow your own guidance if this happens.

All previous steps are simply preparation for this meditation. These are the same steps for each meditation type you will do. The first meditation in our journey will integrate new information from the previous chapter.

Utilize meditations anytime you need to process new information while on this journey. Integration occurs by bringing new information into your cells for assimilation. Once this happens, the energy starts moving out to activate and amend your reality. You will begin working with the root, knee, and foot chakras, which target themes of your destiny, ancestry, and personal potential.

1. As you continue to hum, feel your feet vibrating. Imagine a bright light opening in your feet. Remember, they represent where you have been and where you are going. This represents your destiny. Now, bring awareness to your ankles. Notice information in many forms (shapes, colors, and people) around your ankles and see it integrate into yourself through the light. Then, watch the light turn a beautiful golden color. Sense that you are taking control of your destiny. Acknowledge the importance of your feet for your human experience on both the physical and energetic layers.

2. Take a deep breath and continue to hum, bringing this energy up to your knees. Acknowledge all the ancestors that came

before you so you could be here now in this human body. Remember, the right knee corresponds to masculine ancestors, starting with your dad. The left knee corresponds with your mom and all the feminine ancestors who came before her. Pull in all the experiences with your parents and integrate them in (positive and negative). It is safe. Now, see a bright white light open up as you also imagine countless concentric circles of your ancestors surrounding you, sending you love and appreciation. Let that love land in you, then feel the gratitude for them, their experiences, and their lives. Ask if there is anything they want you to receive to help you on your life's journey. Watch as the information from them comes to your knees. Take a deep breath to allow it in. Then, see the light in your knees shine like two white stars.

3. Next, move the energy and your awareness to your root chakra as you continue to hum. These are your reproductive organs and your genitals. There exists the potential energy for your life's path. See two powerful flames ignite and begin to burn bright and strongly. This fire is your potential and the beginning of your power source. Imagine the fire rising and getting brighter. See your breath feeding the flames. Feel the power of transformation and transcendence in these flames.

4. As the flames grow, they burn everything above them. Spend a minute feeding the fire. Each flame is a part of your internal polarity, and they are beginning to work together to create, transform, and transcend.

## Closing Your Practice

When you feel ready, repeat the physical touch scan all over your body, starting with your head and working to your feet. Move, wiggle, and stretch to complete your practice and finally open your eyes.

Alternatively, keep your eyes closed and sit with the openings and shifts you allow. If you can, sense the subtle energetic openings that have occurred. You may also still feel energy moving and completing its journey. Sit with it till it feels complete.

Journal about new experiences, sensations, or insights you had during or after the meditation. Then, you can continue with your additional practices afterward or engage in them later in the day.

### *Journaling*

As mentioned in the introduction of this book, it will be exceptionally beneficial to keep a journal of your experiences. Note your difficulties, breakthroughs, and questions as they arise during your journey. It is a great way to keep track of your progress, process and understand what is arising in your experiences, and illuminate how events are part of the bigger picture of your growth.

You can also note what practices you like and which ones you struggle with. This chapter offers an extra-juicy practice: the Steps to Change a Pattern. I invite you to journal and track at least one to three applications of this per week.

Louise Hays's book *Emotional Causes of Disease* is helpful to analyzing the purpose of situations and the physical issues you experience. You can find the complete list of conditions and emotions from this book online for free.

During this first round of expansion practices, I invite you to set one or more intentions for your journey throughout this book. Here are a few suggestions that might resonate or help you find your own language:

- *To align and live from my true inner self*
- *To release the density that is holding me back*

- *To live entirely from my fully activated heart space*
- *To evolve my grounding and centeredness so profoundly that I experience joy, Love, and fulfillment as my primary mode of operation*

Next, we introduce your additional practices. Many additional practices throughout this book can be added to the end of your daily meditation. This creates ease with the new patterns and makes those practices accessible throughout daily life.

## Watching the Thinker

The beginning of freedom is realizing that you are not the thinker in your mind. The thinking part of the brain is an evolutionary tool that humans have come to identify themselves with as if their thoughts are who they are. The moment you start watching the thinker, you activate a higher level of consciousness. The awareness connects you to vast intelligence beyond the regular thoughts you can tune into. This opens access to Love, creativity, joy, and inner peace beyond the mind.

1. Start all meditations by readying yourself and your space, completing both breathing exercises (alternate nostril and box breathing), creating safety and comfort practice, and bringing humming through the body as detailed above.

2. Continue the meditation with slow inhales through the nose that fills the belly first. Then, exhale through the nose and match the length of the inhale. Continue this calming flow.

3. Now sit in silence and stillness. As your thoughts arise, watch them as if they are not yours. Put your attention on them as if someone else is saying them. This is the beginning of disassociating who you are from your thinking mind or ego. It is important to remember that the ego is just a tool, not who you really are.

4. Some can connect better by imagining the ruminations playing out on a movie screen or a hamster running on a wheel. Choose whatever works best for you. It is like your awareness moves into the right side of your mind as you watch the left side.

5. Sit here and remain curious about who is watching the thinker. Feel the awareness that exists beyond thought. Connect with a glimmer of excitement for the freedom this is creating.

6. Close your meditation practice as before—Journal about your experience or any new awareness.

This simple act helps you disidentify with your thinking mind while your consciousness sits back and watches all the loops, flips, and pathways your thought process takes. This is called *metacognition*, or the ability to control your thinking, and it's one of our most recent evolutionary advances. It's considered to be something only humans can do through genetic adaptation.

This concept will help you connect to a "felt" experience of watching the thinker before we expand on it in the following chapters. When you become adept at applying this mental flexibility, you will begin to free your mind from autopilot.

Amazingly, our next phase of evolution is happening now, and it will not take millions or even thousands of years of natural selection to implement. You are a part of this present planetary evolution!

Once you can disidentify with your mind, changing patterns becomes more accessible. Try out the next section, where you can practice the steps to revise and transform your behaviors.

## Steps to Change a Pattern

When you're on autopilot, you are operating solely from previous patterns (from your own experience, from your family, or ancestor's).

This robs you of the ability to perceive the different choices available to you. A new choice could lead to new experiences for your growth and enjoyment in your life. It's what keeps you stuck. You can create change in your world through two primary levels.

The first is by changing your patterns of doing throughout the day. Brush your teeth with your left hand instead of your right, walk to the store instead of taking the car, clean the house in the opposite order, or change your morning routine. Breaking your normal patterns gives you access to your awareness and helps you be more present.

*There will always be patterns. They are part of how we follow the flow of life. You are trying to create flexibility to choose new patterns in order to create your life differently.*

How and why do you get stuck in patterns? Once your brain knows how to do something, it becomes almost automatic. Your awareness is not engaged, which allows your brain to conserve energy. But when you engage your awareness, you notice all the options and opportunities you would have otherwise missed. This practice creates new neural connections.

The second change comes from your internal world and is just as important as making changes in your external world, both change the structure of your brain. The Watching the Thinker exercise will allow you to see your automatic reactions as patterns that repeat in your mind, giving you a new power to make different decisions about how you think, respond, and move about your reality.

In general, here are the steps to change a limiting internal pattern:

1. Gain awareness of the pattern. The Watching the Thinker exercise can be helpful here.

2. Maintain awareness of the pattern when it is happening or being triggered.

3. Resist the need to judge that pattern.

4. Identify whether an unmet need is keeping the pattern in play.

5. Find a way to meet that need. Make a different choice when similar situations come up that would have previously triggered the old behavior.

It's a common habit for many people to say they are sorry frequently. An example might be that your next-door neighbor is throwing a party, and the music is too loud. You say, "Sorry, can you please turn down the music?" Or, as another example, maybe you bump into a stranger on the street and apologize.

In these scenarios, you show that you are sorry for existing in some way. Now, it is essential to say you are sorry in a healthy context, but overuse diminishes your power and self-worth. You can still be kind and considerate of others without it. If this is a pattern you have experienced, simply take *sorry* out of the sentence.

At this point, the first step is accomplished! You have identified the pattern that diminishes the self. Next is trying to catch the behavior in the moment, as saying sorry has likely become a reflex in many situations. It is okay for it to slip out sometimes still. Although this step is about noticing and being curious about its disempowering nature, the third step is all about not judging the pattern once you have identified it.

Sometimes, that is all it takes to change a pattern and make a new behavioral choice. Other times, the juicy, deeply wired patterns may fill a long-term unmet need. Some digging might be needed here. In our sorry example from above, it's possible that you felt your parents did not have enough time for you as a child. Maybe you felt like a burden to them. Whether it is true or not doesn't matter, as this perception came during an impressionable time. Afterward, you develop behaviors in response to keep yourself safe.

Fast-forward to the present time and overusing the word *sorry*—now you know precisely where that behavior came from, which might be enough to help you change the pattern through awareness. However, you may still need to shift something to feel more empowered and worthy.

You can add this to your daily meditations if you are drawn to it. Journal to reflect on any insights or interesting experiences this or any of the exercises reveal to you.

## Movement

Movement is an indispensable element in caring for your human machinery, as it combines physical purification and optimization to complement the mental purification you're working toward. Fanning the fires of your metabolism will support your processes to break down old mental patterns and create something new. You get to choose what this looks like for you, and as always, consult your doctor before changing your fitness routine.

You don't have to become a marathon runner or an aerobics junkie if you don't want to. If you don't currently have a movement practice or find you are doing something you no longer enjoy, bring the fun back to movement and find something you like.

*A key attribute to making the most of moving is to be present in that movement and to enjoy it. Connect with your body and the joy of simply being able to move!*

You have heard the adage, *Your body is a temple,* and that is precisely why you are engaging in conscious movement—treating this physical form like the sacred vessel it is. Use this perspective to inspire your practice.

The magic number for the body is movement at least three times per week. It is desirable to engage in something daily, even if it is a short walk.

If you prefer lower-intensity activity, consider the following:

- Restorative yoga or yin yoga
- Tai chi
- Qi gong
- Walks in nature
- Ecstatic dance
- Kundalini yoga (which is more of a breathing practice than a traditional yoga practice)
- Light weightlifting

If you do a lot of sitting during the day, get up and sneak in movement breaks. This gets the energy flowing and makes cognition and the day go better.

If you prefer high-intensity activity, you may already have some movement you like engaging in. However, it is great to change it up and get some variety. Here are suggestions for you:

- Brisk walking with hills
- More-intense yoga (e.g., hot yoga, Bikram yoga, vinyasa yoga)
- Cardio training (e.g., running, stair step machine, elliptical machine)
- Pilates
- Aerobic group classes
- Weightlifting
- Dancing (swing, line, hula, etc.)

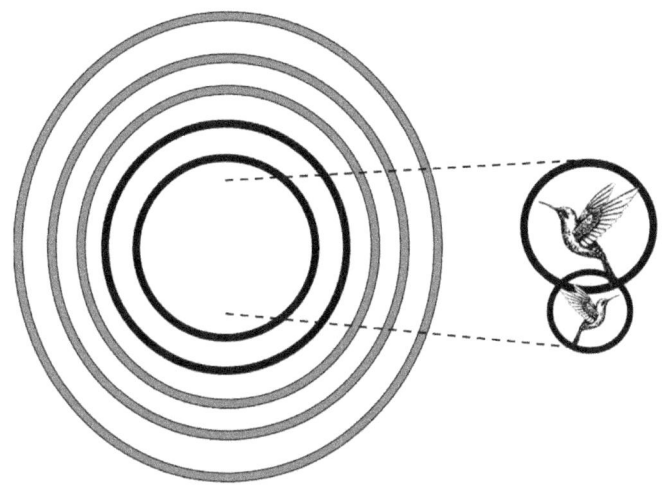

# Second Octave:
# Chapters 3 and 4

### Awareness of Your Emotional Technology
### (Physical Plane)

You are responsible for your emotions. Your emotions are the chemical gateway to spiritual transformation and maturation.

**Old Perspective:** *An unconscious directive, as in "I feel misunderstood and struggle to get my needs met by others."*

**New Perspective:** *A conscious engagement, as in "My experience of reality is my creation."*

# CHAPTER 3

# Love, Hormones, and Emotions

*Hormones are the vehicle for the embodiment of spirit.*

—Stuart Sovatsky

Love is the creation of health in the body through connection with yourself, others, and the wider world.

Chapter 1 depicts how hormones have evolved to drive mammals together for reproduction, familial organization, and communal cooperation. This chapter will further explore how hormones make you feel and how they relate to experiences of love. Hormones are also a valuable metric in love research because they are observable and quantifiable.

These molecules can be powerful healers in our physiology: they don't just make you feel good; they create health in the body. States of connectedness, joy, and peace gained from these hormones can be our everyday baseline in life. All emotions create energy and movement within the body. Can you imagine the difference between the energy created by Love versus an emotion like fear?

## The Healing Power of Connection

My experience highlights the importance of connection to others, yourself, and the natural world. I have spent large chunks of my life single, and these were the times I struggled the most with my health. For example, at thirty, I was three years post-divorce and had sworn off relationships because I wanted to focus on my career. Indeed, I accomplished a great deal during this time, including completing a Ph.D., traveling, giving talks, presenting research, and remodeling a house.

I enjoyed this period, but work was my main focus, often excluding time outdoors and with friends. I also largely self-identified with my work, and my health began to deteriorate. My response was to ignore what my body was trying to bring to my attention to and push forward—big mistake!

I slowly got better over the years, but what helped me make the most significant shift toward healing was an exceptionally loving, connected, and supportive relationship. It was like ten years of healing in *one* year! These hormones are so much more than something that makes you feel good. They are a key to health and longevity. This is something we can cultivate both within ourselves and through connections with others.

This chapter will also explore how subconscious feelings of separation are essential areas to bring awareness. Leading to re-engagement of the connectedness that circulates health-generating hormones. Also, this lays a foundation for the more spiritual connections we'll explore in chapters 7 and 9.

Of course, just because you are in a relationship does not mean you are experiencing these feelings and hormones. It concerns how separate you have become from the other person and yourself. An awareness is needed to better understand how separation affects your experience.

Also, it's important to note that you can learn how to stimulate these hormones with your own emotions. Most people wait for something to happen to feel good, like eating chocolate or even buying something new—the extreme of which can lead to more addictive behaviors. However, this feeling of gratification is only temporary and will soon wear away, leaving one feeling empty or even craving more.

The tragic thing is this dysfunction can also become one's baseline. To combat this, there is a gratitude exercise in the next chapter's expansion practices to begin to help you nurture a new baseline state. Let's start with understanding how hormones can support our health.

The idea has been popularized that stress (and the subsequent cascade of stress hormones) is a major contributor to many diseases. Furthermore, it is evident that when chronic stress is experienced, quality of life deteriorates, but when there are expanding feelings (happiness, contentment, joy, etc.), quality of life improves.

This raises the question: What are the specific physical implications of positive hormones on health? How do you cultivate these positive hormones to improve your quality of life and health? Let's first consider the significant effect of hormones on health, then build perspectives and practices throughout the rest of the book to help increase your experience of them.

## How Hormones Affect Health

Many research studies examine how administering different hormones correlates with observed physiological changes. While this may be an accurate way to study the effects of these hormones, the "magic pill" approach is not a reasonable long-term solution. The purpose of these systems is described below to display the profound intelligence of the human body. Your body is a miracle of homeostasis!

*Homeostasis means your body constantly responds to your internal and external circumstances to optimize its function.*

This is *every-body's* primary mode of operation. When something falls out of balance, there is a reason for it. Instead of reaching for a supplement to accommodate the chemical you are low in, ask yourself, "Why am I low in the first place?"

Supplement usage, you might say, is a natural way to support your hormones for healthy homeostasis. While this is a natural approach, I argue it still has the potential to negate your body's capabilities. Instead of increasing your supplements, increase your connection with yourself and others to give you exactly what you need to maintain a healthful state.

I believe supplementation should be reserved for short-term application, potentially to show an individual what the feeling is, or in long-term cases where all other solutions have been exhausted. However, consult your doctor before changing your medications or supplements, and monitor hormone levels via testing.

Here, I'll introduce oxytocin, dopamine, and serotonin. There are complicated interrelationships between hormones. For example, testosterone has been observed to upregulate dopamine, while serotonin has a long-observed effect on estrogen utilization. Further, progesterone is correlated with regulating gamma-aminobutyric acid, an inhibitory molecule known to have a calming effect on the nervous system.

All these hormones interact in ways that are not described here or fully understood at this time. However, we will develop an appreciation for these molecules through our discussion, revealing a new relationship and understanding of your body. To begin, let's discuss dopamine.

## Dopamine

Dopamine is one of the main hormones that helps us feel pleasure in the human experience. Physiologically, it has been observed to play a role in movement, heart rate, digestion, kidney function, sleep, pain processing, blood vessel function, and even pancreatic and insulin regulation. It is part of the brain's reward system, so it reinforces behaviors when it is secreted. While this can be harnessed for good, it also means that negative behaviors can create patterns of addiction.

Now, let's consider dopamine's utility in supporting health. Studies have shown that both the kidneys and the heart have dopamine receptors, which is why dopamine has been used to treat congestive heart failure and kidney issues. In the kidneys, these receptors also regulate electrolyte secretion.

Furthermore, it has been observed that dopamine can decrease insulin and support glucose homeostasis, though its exact mechanism still needs to be understood. Additionally, dopamine is a natural analgesic that inhibits pain. This is why many with Parkinson's disease, which is associated with lowered levels of dopamine, report having a lot of pain. The same is true for individuals with fibromyalgia and restless leg syndrome.

There are likely many other positive effects of dopamine on the body not listed here. I share these few to demonstrate the necessity of a balanced health and well-being hormone system.

This discussion of dopamine would be incomplete without also mentioning addiction. Addiction occurs when people use a substance or a thing to create feel-good hormones that they otherwise have difficulty accessing. Gabor Mate is a retired physician and bestselling author on the topic of addiction who defines *addiction* as "craving pleasure, and relief in the short term, negative consequences in the long term, and the ability or refusal to desist."

It doesn't matter what the addiction is; it's all the same issue. Drug addicts, gamblers, and hoarders all get dopamine hits that drive their destructive behaviors. The crux is that they *seemingly* cannot create these feel-good hormones independently and need something external to feed those basic human needs.

When in a cycle of addiction, there is a feeling of emptiness that drives the need for more after the last hit of dopamine wears off. Over time, these addictions can dysregulate the normal homeostatic feedback mechanisms of the body, after which it gets even more challenging to obtain the high or reward feeling.

There are many other things you can be addicted to, but each one is a symptom of the same issue: difficulty connecting to both your deeper self and to others. If you are genuinely connected to yourself and others, there is little need to seek anything else because these feel-good hormones will create a sense of fulfillment naturally.

Many people may not realize that they are experiencing an addiction pattern. Some common examples include addiction to food, video games, buying things, or even caffeine. Some addictions are considered more acceptable than others in our culture, like sugar addiction. However, they all carry consequences in pattern development that can often seem unrelated and impair hormone regulation.

Do you depend on a quick fix to make you feel better? If so, realize that you might be craving a connection with others. Something as benign as chocolate (that was mine!), when consumed habitually for its feel-good properties, can signal that you need more connection.

## Serotonin

Serotonin is an essential hormone in the regulation of mood. In addition to supporting mood, serotonin has fifteen known receptors in the brain and elsewhere in the body. It has been observed to regulate the cardiovascular system, bowel motility, bladder control, and even platelet aggregation in the blood. In the human experience, balanced serotonin correlates with well-being and happiness.

Pharmaceutical companies have focused on drugs that increase the availability of serotonin to treat depression. However, as advantageous as these seem, there are often side effects to this class of drugs that also make it difficult to discontinue their use. This is due to homeostatic mechanisms; when you take a substance that increases serotonin availability, your body will lower its natural production.

You should thank your body for this because too much can cause serotonin syndrome, a potentially fatal condition. Furthermore, many medications that target depression do not allow for regular daily ups and downs, often leading to a feeling of disconnection or numbness to the world. Although there are situations when this is needed, it is not a long-term solution for most people.

For many people, disconnection is what creates depression in the first place. It is my opinion that the overuse of antidepressants could potentially inhibit the natural expansion of consciousness in some individuals. Everyone has their path from separation to awareness and connection; every hardship endured is a potential vector for your healing. This is the work! Doing the work is always rewarded with an expanded experience of emotions and perspectives that improve your life.

## Oxytocin

Oxytocin, released by the hypothalamus and pituitary glands, is the driver of feeling connected to others and the world. However, science is now realizing it has a much more significant role in our health. One example is that oxytocin helps heal heart tissue, previously thought impossible for the body to regenerate.

Dr. Altor Aguirre is an assistant professor of biomedical engineering at the University of Michigan whose research has uncovered a link between healing heart tissue and oxytocin in animal models. He observed that oxytocin reprograms the outer layer of heart cells to become stem cells.

Stem cells can become any other type of cells needed during the healing process. These outer-layer stem cells can migrate all the way to the inner layers of the heart, or wherever the damage is. Stem cells replace damaged heart vessels, cells, and more structural connective tissue.

Furthermore, the importance of a healthy gut microbiome in relation to other bodily systems has grown in widespread knowledge. Your microbiome is the total population of different bacteria strains and microorganisms in your gut that helps digest your food.

In laboratory models, mice were fed a probiotic derived from human breast milk, which stimulated oxytocin. The effect continued to also lower stress hormones via the HPA (hypothalamic-pituitary-adrenal) axis.

There is also evidence that healthy oxytocin levels lower wound-healing time and inflammation. It is an essential factor to manage since it is present in all disease states and is part of their cause and progression. Also remarkable is oxytocin's observed ability to regulate food intake and body weight.

In fact, researchers are looking to develop drugs that increase oxytocin for weight loss purposes. What if a key cause of obesity is feelings of deep disconnection, leading the body to produce insufficient levels of oxytocin? There can be many reasons why oxytocin is low, but if the source is emotional, an increased connection with others may likely be a viable remedy.

If the true purpose of hormones is to support health and a deeper state of human experience, the initial source of dysfunction must be rooted in separation. This would even affect epigenetic issues, as the regulation of your DNA is responsible for the creation and reception of hormones.

## Your Experience Changes Your Gene Expression!

*Experience: This is your individual understanding of reality, built through perceptions and beliefs. Likewise, your experiences feed these perceptions and beliefs.*

What is epigenetics? Your epigenome is the most impressive homeo-static regulatory system in your body! Your DNA contains all the instructions on how to run your body, and epigenetics regulates that.

Epigenetic mechanisms decide which genetic instructions get read and which are ignored, and it all starts at conception. While in your mother's womb, you were responding to how she felt about the outside environment to prepare for the type of world you would enter.

This means that quite literally everything you have ever thought, felt, or consumed has impacted your genes through epigenetic regulation. DNA and RNA are the hardware that establishes how cells respond to the inner and outer environments of the body—a process that occurs through the actions of proteins.

The comprehensive nature of epigenetic feedback determines our reactions to disease, who we are, and what we will become. When ideal inputs (food, emotions, beliefs, etc.) are given to the human system on multiple levels, optimal regulation of the body becomes possible.

You might ask how epigenetics is affected by thoughts and beliefs. Well, senses are the nervous system's means of helping organisms interact with their environments and are closely tied to emotion. Thoughts and beliefs are the brain's way of understanding sensory inputs concerning what is going on in the world around us.

Such sensations can be interpreted as an approximation rather than truth, especially since past experiences can impact emotional responses. This approximation profoundly impacts one's epigenetics, as it creates a field of information, which means that it impacts genetic transcriptions and, by extension, one's physiology.

> *Furthermore, this means a direct connection exists between a person's consciousness and the proteins that regulate all the body's functions. This is your own personal metamorphic field that you create.*

## Emotions, Epigenetics, and the Body

It is well established that prenatal stress and early childhood trauma can expose epigenomes to emotional regulation issues, such as trouble managing stress or even difficulties with addiction later in life. One study suggests that even nightmares from severe traumatic events can be epigenetically inherited from previous generations.

Suppose a pregnant mother experiences high levels of stress. In that case, the baby's epigenome catalogs the outside world as stressful and shifts nervous system development to accommodate being born into a stressful environment. This has been observed to affect the baby's immune system, metabolism, and even brain development permanently and negatively.

Think about the last time you were genuinely stressed. Most people, when stressed, feel disconnected from themselves, their environment, and other people around them. Some live constantly in this place and are in a permanent state of fight or flight. Imagine what this might do to your genetic regulation and hormone levels.

Even as an adult, regularly having strong negative emotional responses can take energy away from essential processes like healing physical wounds. Negative emotions can be defined as unpleasant reactions to a situation, which I often describe as a contracting emotion.

One 2007 study showed that when subjects were angry, stem cells received a weaker message to heal their ailments because the body's resources were focused on building threat-response biochemicals. Imagine what this does to the body in the long term when anger is repressed and ignored.

In such cases, the emotional signals essentially overpowered the repair signals; this demonstrates how information from the nervous system uses epigenetic changes to shift energy from one system to another via the regulation of DNA. It only takes one regulatory gene to drive input into roughly one thousand other genes, and what informs that initial gene can be as simple as one thought, emotion, or belief.

Each person is a walking web of acquired beliefs. Many of these beliefs, however, are outdated and actively create a contradiction somewhere in our physiologies. As an adult, for example, do you still believe the fear you gained at six years old about clowns being evil? When you didn't feel safe, your mind created that belief within seconds, then stored the pattern for future recognition.

The result is that the next time you see a clown, which you once identified as a dangerous entity, your nervous system alerts you to keep you safe. This has practical applications when encountering dangerous situations, but subconsciously, you don't need to hold on to every reaction.

The problem is that these previously established beliefs are often never reviewed to determine whether they are outdated, so the brain continues to retain them. Two of the most common subconscious beliefs I encounter in my work are "I am not good enough" and "There is something wrong with me."

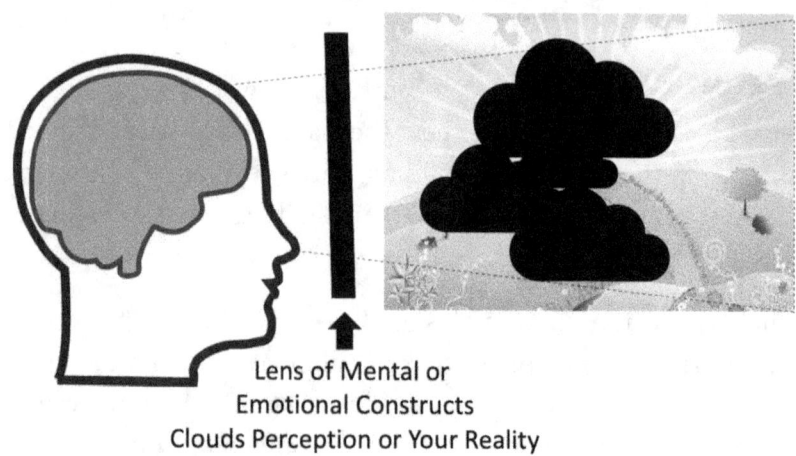

**Lens of Mental or
Emotional Constructs
Clouds Perception or Your Reality**

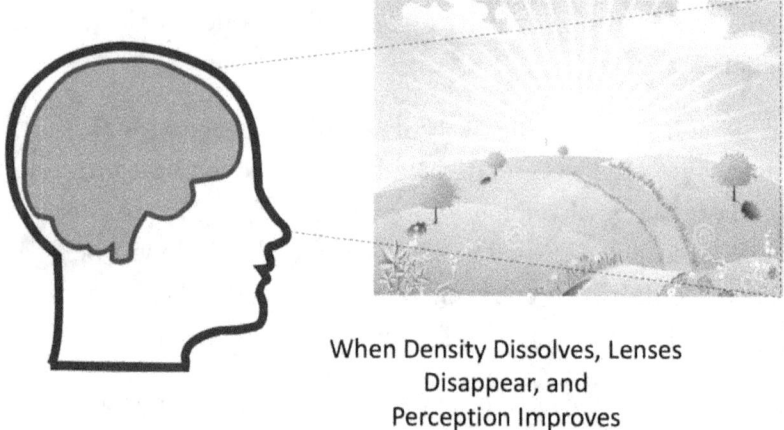

**When Density Dissolves, Lenses
Disappear, and
Perception Improves**

The above image shows what happens when acquired belief systems cloud our view of reality and impact our experience. This is akin to wearing glasses with lenses that obscure the world around you; only you don't know you are wearing them! This lack of accurate vision can lead to more contracted feelings about yourself and the world.

When that density dissolves, you can begin to perceive reality in its fullness and not only see but take the opportunities you would have previously never imagined.

Furthermore, embodying strongly internalized beliefs can not only negatively influence life experiences but also change how genes are transcribed. Now, you can see some of the ways that you can create internal mechanisms that keep you separated from others and even yourself. Everyone struggles to feel love when they are in separation or duality consciousness.

A 2007 Harvard study by Dr. Alia Crum found that mindset and established beliefs significantly affect a person's health. One researcher invited a group of eighty-eight maids to a study. Dr. Crum told half of them that the work they do is excellent exercise; the other half was her control group, so she said nothing.

Over the next thirty days, the first group reported weight loss and lower blood pressure, while the second group had no changes. This shows the power that mindset has on your physiology. While not specified in the study, consider that this outcome was potentially driven by epigenetic mechanisms fueled by a change in established beliefs.

You have so much more power over your reality than you think! Start believing that you are an amazing creation of homeostasis with control over your experience. It is true whether you are consciously aware of it or not, and it is beneficial to be conscious of your superpowers!

As we discussed, the concept of metamorphic fields being the facilitator between genetics and evolution is credited to Scott Gilbert. I believe there is a confluence between an individual's consciousness (when engaged), their environment, and metamorphic fields that can put the individual in the driver's seat of their evolution. This is the heart of the superpower we are developing through the technology of our body.

Adopting this perspective can shift your mindset and intention-ally create more joy and purpose in your life. This will also change the physiology of your body. Next, we will introduce a behavioral description of all the main hormones associated with love. These felt sensations are central to establishing a deeper connection between your human self and what you are beyond.

## Love Hormones and Human Behavior

There are eleven main hormones associated with love. For our pur-poses, nine of the eleven will be explored to familiarize you with how these love hormones drive human behavior in the context of romantic love. They all, of course, have a place in both our previous and future evolutions.

Therefore, cultivating an expanded sense of these hormones is part of our journey in this book. You don't have to be in a romantic relationship to remember these feelings and activate their release. I invite you to read each description and connect it to a memory of the feeling as if you are experiencing it now. If you cannot connect to a particular hormone, imagine a situation where you would.

> *This deep remembering of your physiology invites more awareness and healing. Most people exist in life as disembodied minds in a physical vehicle. However, you are an embodied spirit in a technology that constantly responds to your internal and external environments through emotions and senses. Connecting with your senses brings you into your body and the present moment deepening your experience.*

It is worth noting which hormones are more challenging to connect with to focus future cultivation in your life. Even watching certain movies can help us experience some of these feelings through our mirroring of the emotions that we observe.

The following hormone descriptions are taken from *Principia Amoris: The New Science of Love* by Dr. John Gottman. This list focuses on how each hormone is experienced in relation to romantic involvement.

I've included the hormones already introduced to give a more in-depth understanding of when you might be feeling their rush. As you read about each one, remember a time or a situation when you experienced each hormone and how it made you feel. This is a valuable exercise to get to know each hormone better. It helped me learn why I love chocolate so much!

| Hormone | Mental/Emotional Experience | Other Information |
|---|---|---|
| Dehydroepiandrosterone (DHEA) | Aphrodisiac; directly excites the sexual centers of the brain | Made from cholesterol in the body and is considered the "mother of all hormones"; affects how the skin feels and looks; increases blood flow to the lips, breasts, and genitals |
| Dopamine | Inspiration, joy, excitement; recognize seek and recognize pleasure | Drives one toward pleasureful experiences |
| Estrogen | Creates an availability in women; increases cognition and balances mood | Contributes to body odor that attracts a mate and supple skin texture |
| Oxytocin | Secreted when we feel close to someone; feeling of wanting to be held | Heightened by touch and cuddling; facilitates birth and milk production in mothers; secreted by the pituitary gland and stimulates the release of dopamine, estrogen, vasopressin, etc.; correlated with poor judgment |

| Hormone | Mental/Emotional Experience | Other Information |
|---------|------------------------------|--------------------|
| Phenylethyl-amine (PEA) | Thrill of falling in love; energizing | Occurs naturally in chocolate |
| Pheromones | Influences sensuality; feelings of well-being and comfort; attraction to potential partner | Produced from DHEA; creates a unique smell that attracts a mate |
| Serotonin | Sexual excitation; calm and warm sociability | More influence on women |
| Testosterone | "Hormone of desire"; lust in both sexes | Increases sexual fantasies; drives behavior toward seeking a sexual partner |
| Vasopressin | Known as the male-bonding hormone; the "molecule of monogamy"; feeling of wanting to stay home; increases immunity and cognition; brings you to the present moment | Active during REM sleep and with theta brain waves |

During the traditional romance of "falling in love," you participate in a cascade of hormones that drive behavior. This is often referred to as Phase 1, and it includes a myriad of different parts of the love system that are connected and feed into one another. Gottam writes:

Phase 1 is a complex mix of affection, soft receptivity, calm sociability, comfort and cuddling, unbridled excitement, the thrill of falling in love, obsessive thinking about the loved one, heightened eagerness and desire, compulsion, electrifying exhilaration, anticipation that something wonderful is happening or about to happen, the seeking of intense pleasure, dreaming about the future together, obsessiveness about the other person, comfort and familiarity, and ease and relating and talking, delight, playfulness, humor, and laughter, aggressive lust, passive and open receptivity, sexual arousal and orgasm, roaming for adventure, a desire to deepen one relationship and stay home, intense interest and absorption with love itself, a feeling that you can really be yourself, acceptance of the partner, delight, comfort, secure bonding and attachment, friendship, fear of rejection and loss, and restlessness, mixed with poor judgment and clouded reasoning.

You can see how Phase 1 of romantic love is a dance of all these hormones. No wonder there is such a drive within humanity to experience it! This initial phase has so much fun, excitement, and expansion. If two people stay together, Phase 2 will, at some point, begin. This phase, which is heavily focused on building trust, usually happens after some commitment, such as when a couple decides to be exclusive, moves in together, or marries. Phase 2 often begins with questioning whether or not you are in the right relationship for you.

I theorize that this could be due to a shift in oxytocin secretion. Again, it is commonly reported that it is easy to ignore red flags and struggle with poor judgment early in a relationship, potentially due to high oxytocin levels. Then, in Phase 2, you must work to maintain the connection and keep the oxytocin flowing.

A lack of this connecting hormone can lead to conflict in Phase 2 because the two individuals are exploring how to establish deeper trust and get more "real" with each other. This is another area where separation can get in the way of connecting with others and the healthful circulation of hormones. Stuck emotions could significantly block your experience of expanded feelings and health-promoting hormones. The first step in unsticking yourself lies in a deeper understanding of polarity and its place in your experience.

## Polarity:
## An Important Theme to Understand

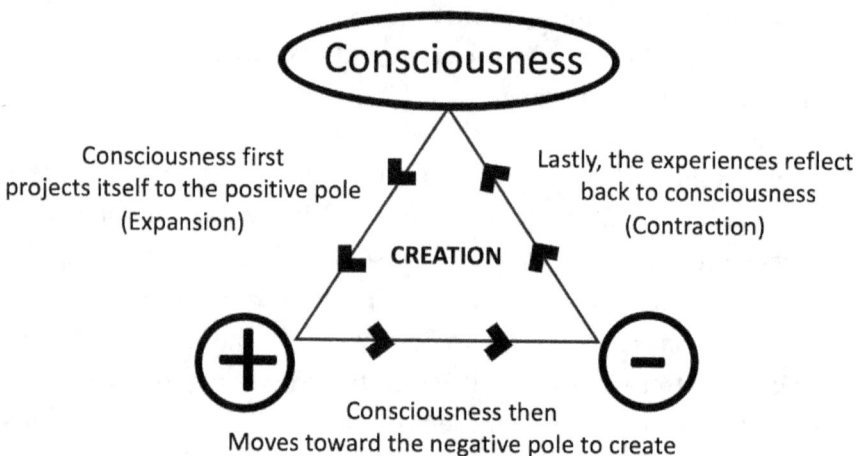

You can think of polarity as light and dark, expansion and contraction, masculine and feminine principles, creation and destruction, or positive and negative. This is the dual nature that, with consciousness, constructs everything within the universe, from the nebula and black holes to the quarks that make up the protons in your body and everything in between. An inherent charge and fields help direct the assembly of matter.

Spirit, metamorphic fields, and consciousness all contribute. This concept applies to everything above and below creation and everywhere in between in the diagram above. The Creator of All constantly manifests reality through the poles, while you, also a creator, manifest your reality through endless expansion and contraction processes.

This is the basic concept of evolution inherent in the universe's design.

*As applied to our daily lives, the most important concept of polarity is that both extremes are of equal benefit. There is no real "bad" or "good," just choices as tools for you to grow.*

Once you have this awareness, you can begin creating *with* the polarity instead of from the consciousness of duality. When in duality, you don't understand why "bad" things happen to you and feel powerless and victimized by life. This can be experienced as subtle subconscious programs or, more obviously, through your conscious thoughts and the words you say.

Reality in all its facets of your body, other people, places, and things constantly reflects how you can improve, grow, and evolve. For the natural universe, no movement is death. Now you can begin to see conflict or crisis as a natural movement to enhance your life.

*Your relationship to duality consciousness determines the level of suffering you experience as a human.*

This perspective takes some time to understand, soften to, and practice. It is also the fundamental reason why everything you have experienced has happened for you, not to you. The complex emotions that arise in the face of challenging situations, such as fear, jealousy, or anger, are what I call *contractions*. Experiencing contractions simply signifies an opportunity for growth in perspective and awareness of where you are experiencing separation.

One example is how stagnation occurs in nature until there is a stimulating force of change. The changing of the seasons can be an example. When all is bleak and empty in winter, the days slowly get longer, and the green leaves poke up from the ground.

This is the feminine principle of winter and nature waiting for the masculine force of the sun to come in and bring change. These are the metamorphic principles at work, and the concept of habit or memory governs this field and keeps spring coming each year.

This polarity exists at every level of your experience, down to the cells that make up your body. Your cells reproduce at a rate of 3.8 million cells per second! Through metamorphic fields and mitosis, one cell becomes two. The ability to reproduce is a fundamental characteristic of being alive.

That describes polarity in matter (the physical), but what about polarity at the emotional level? Duality consciousness creates emotional separation from the unintegrated ego. Since the purpose of this part of your brain is to act as an internal alarm system, it can create contracted emotions through the limbic system.

This signal then travels through your nervous system to affect physiology, hormones, and organ systems. There is nothing wrong with having contracted emotions. How you deal with the signals creates your experience and with awareness you can make consciousness choices here. They are always presenting an opportunity for information and growth.

It is common for the contracting emotion to be ignored or overridden, which creates incoherence within the system. Then, the emotion creates density and gets deposited in an area of the body. When this happens, the opportunity to expand *after* contraction is missed! The good news is that it can always be reexperienced and moved through. This is where growth happens. In the next chapter's expansion practices, we begin to explore this.

You will meet people and situations throughout life trying to help you bring these contracted emotions back up to move them. Some of what you may think of as your greatest enemies or most difficult relationships are challenging for this reason.

After you shift perspectives, you will learn to greet contractions with excitement because you will know that each signifies an opportunity for growth. This way of being does not allow victimhood and gives you the power to reflect and learn from a situation quickly. Then, in the future, you have the awareness to choose one pole or the other for growth. The negative pole will likely always be part of human development. Although, the relationship to it can change as awareness grows and you pull yourself out of duality consciousness.

Your entire existence is a beautiful dance of polarity. Once you engage it consciously, you begin to release density to create with yourself and the metamorphic fields. It's here that a deep integration occurs; it's the beginning of self-maturation and true manifestation.

It is waiting for you to engage. In your world, you are directing your experience either consciously or unconsciously. As you come more deeply into creatorship (conscious creation) in your life, you will be eager to engage with polarity as the two sides that come together to create what is.

Now that you have the perspectives that open your ability to move through stuck emotions and difficult dynamics, the full liberating force becomes forgiveness.

## Forgiveness as Healing, Opening to Your Being

When we harbor resentments and negative feelings toward others to blame them for our suffering, it only creates problems for us and keeps us in duality consciousness. It also represents a situation that has not been well integrated and, therefore, continues to plague and limit us if we are the ones who feel "wronged" by another. This is a critical aspect of integrating your life experiences: learning to forgive yourself and others for perceived wrongs.

This is some of the most challenging work you can do because you must go above the "story" of the situation and the ego reaction programmed to keep you safe. Writing or journaling about the situation or your perception and experience of what happened is useful. This is what runs in your mind unconsciously and may be keeping you in a limbic system loop.

When you write it down, you can bring further awareness to different aspects of the situation and observe it from a third-person viewpoint. Forgiveness can become an option once you have some mental and emotional perspective.

Talking out your story with someone can be helpful. However, unconsciously speaking and writing your story is not. For example, you may know a friend or relative who tells the same story repeatedly about how someone wronged them. They are stuck in an unconscious loop and go over the story because they feel victimized and seek your validation.

The focus should not be on the story itself but on analyzing what the situation was trying to teach you. All that you experience is a mirror for your growth. The ego in the mind will most likely be triggered if this is a newer conscious practice, as this part of the self feels hurt in these situations.

If you find yourself triggered as you talk or write, you can use the strength of your reaction as a barometer of how strong your resistance to change is. In a Watching the Thinker fashion, find it interesting and stay curious. If you find yourself frequently hurt or offended by others, this indicates that this part of your mind is strong.

*Many spiritual traditions suggest that initiates deliberately attract negative attention and criticism to eventually "weaken" their ego in order to evolve.*

This is not necessarily needed if you can bring awareness to when it is happening, and instead of identifying with the story, notice the mind's reaction and thank it for letting you know that there is an unhealed part of yourself. What is paramount to remember is that you are not forgiving others to let them off the hook—you are forgiving them to free yourself!

Look at it this way: when you hold onto negative feelings, you are not actually affecting the other person, only punishing yourself. Once you realize this, you become aware of the power of forgiveness to truly change your life.

Forgiveness feeds directly into the themes of the sacral chakra, which we will talk about next. Each chakra needs energy flow to operate optimally on the physical, emotional, and spiritual levels. This optimization takes your conscious awareness.

## Sacral Chakra: I Feel

The second chakra, the sacral chakra, is behind the belly button. This chakra correlates with an orange frequency of light, feminine polarity, and the element of water. Its endocrine organs (which create hormones) include the adrenals and the womb in women and the womb space in men.

The adrenals make energy for the body through hormonal secretions like cortisol and adrenaline, both of which create energy and a drive in the body. This is the chakra of energy and creation.

The themes of this chakra directly relate to the creation and movement of energy. Creation is always two poles coming together to make something new. That is why this chakra is often correlated with sexuality. Although, it is not just about the creation of life (children) but also with all that you will create in your world.

The sacral chakra is such a powerful center of creation that this is where your subsequent evolutions will be first generated, depending on the inputs from your environment, your resulting emotions, and whether you let the energy move. This is either creation or destruction; both are needed for life and evolution.

This creation energy is also at the center of every atom in you and existence. The center of the universe exists in each atom, and all is within you!

As far as love is concerned, this chakra brings in the emotional component of how you relate to yourself as a being of Love and how you give Love to create in the world. It all starts with letting the energy move and optimizing what is being created. Much of your energy is created through eating, assimilating, and digesting food. Therefore, ensuring your inputs are aligned and your digestion is functioning well is a fundamental facet of support for the sacral chakra.

While this chakra is activated by energy from the adrenals atop the kidneys, frustrations, and fears can become lodged in the kidneys and block the flow of energy. Relationally, this chakra is themed on how you treat yourself and how that extends to how you treat others. This includes your ability to forgive, give Love, have compassion, and acceptance. If you can't provide these things to yourself, your ability to hold them for others is greatly diminished.

To balance this chakra, let your feelings about yourself move through you, whether negative or positive. Awareness and movement of these emotions generates usable energy for both you and the universe.

There are no good or bad emotions, only different energies and frequencies. The goal is to find harmony and balance between the feelings and let them keep moving.

*Harmony of our inner creator is the mastery of self and maturation that this journey is moving you toward.*

*This does not occur by ignoring, shutting down, or controlling emotions. You must bring awareness to understand each emotion and where it comes from. All emotions have come from experiences or even the food we eat.*

If you would like to raise the frequency of the energy moving through your second chakra, work on forgiving, having gratitude for your experiences, appreciating yourself, improving the quality of food you eat, and your digestion. There are forgiveness and polarity expansion practices in the next chapter.

The key to appreciating yourself is acknowledging your strengths. Treat them as if they're your superpowers. Then, you can view your perceived weaknesses simply as opportunities to learn and develop new superpowers.

Practicing this expanded perspective is helpful because it saves you from identifying weaknesses with who you are. You may be stuck in a pattern, but it is not who you are. The balancing side of that perspective is cultivating a perception of the deep beauty in the human experience.

Anything you use to try to escape from relationships—not being honest, being overly focused on work, not connecting with your closest human relationships, and even using technology like television, phones, and computers—blocks the energy flow of this chakra. Anything that takes you out of the present moment creates increased separation.

This takes you out of relating to yourself and others. Using sex as a distraction or an addiction can also block this energy and create more feelings of unfulfillment. These diversions are not the path to the genuine interpersonal connection that humans seek. Fear and emotional immaturity are ultimately two of the most common things that block this chakra.

Instead of perceiving conflicts and difficulties happening around you, start to perceive it all as a beautiful dance of polarity as you and the universe create. This creation is art! You shift your position as you bring awareness to reality's truer nature. You realize it is not trying to destroy you but creating with you.

Within the sacral chakra is also the opportunity to connect with the natural world. This chakra is formed when you are in your mother's womb and before your spirit and mind incarnate. There is an instinctive connection here between your physical body and your greater surroundings.

It is associated with the right side of the brain and an unconscious connection to the themes above. Balance this chakra by being creative. You can take a contracted emotion and move that energy by creating art, redecorating a room in your home, or doing anything that engages the right brain with creation. Alternatively, you can connect to nature with a present and empty mind. Feel the harmony and oneness that you are a part of!

## Chapter Recap

### Illuminated Takeaway

*You are learning the secrets of how to fully operate your human body's technology. This chapter unveils an additional level at which you can create internal homeostasis via the experience of hormones and connection. This begins to lift and open your reality.*

Science suggests that love and the cascade of hormones it presents is an evolutionary strategy for survival and points to the importance of connection with others as mammals—primarily partners, children, and other family members.

Your body's machinery is listening for signals from your emotions and dramatically affects how your physiology runs, down to your DNA. The human body is programmed to need many of these love hormones for health and well-being, as they support the emotional and physical quality of life.

It is essential to understand that this is only part of what love fully is. Chapter 1 presented perspectives on how our past evolution has humanity poised for a quantum leap in conscious evolution. In this chapter, we learned how hormones are needed for homeostasis in your body. Feelings of love, gratitude, and connection create these hormones, generate health, improve your experience, and open the door for further expansion.

But there is more! In the following chapters, there are other steps to learn to balance the mind, which then opens access to the glorious technology of your heart. In chapter 5, we will see that your mind and perceptions directly affect your emotional experience and that you can consciously regulate them.

Then, you will begin to consider how capital *L* Love is also our true nature beyond this human experience and the key to our full embodiment and evolution in these bodies. We are inching toward remembering Love more fully.

It's time for another round of expansion practices!

**At this point in your journey, you may begin to experience or feel . . .**

- New perspectives that create awareness of the importance of connection and the circulation of hormones in the human experience
- A curiosity about how you might increase your felt sense (and therefore your secretion) of the hormones described in this chapter
- Awe at the incredible technology of the human body and its physiologic evolution that marries experience with health

# CHAPTER 4

# Expansion Practices for the Emotional Body

A t this point, you understand the interconnectedness of emo-tions, the creation of energy, hormones, and health in the body. At the higher level, we are truly building the vehicle for the full human embodiment of the spirit.

The expansion exercises during your second month aim to connect you to an expanded experience of gratitude and the resulting hor-mones it brings to your body. From there, chakra sound meditations will activate the sacral chakra to clarify themes of this energy center.

At this point in your journey, you should begin to experience:

- The power of emotions
- More self-mastery over your emotions
- Access to more expanded emotional depth (like forgiveness and awe) in your daily life
- Access to more senses in the body

As always, practice the new exercises for a minimum of four weeks.

## Practice Overview and Checklist

### Daily Meditation

- Add in sacral chakra humming to your daily meditation practice, detailed below.
- Rotate altering your daily meditation to include one of the new additional practices: Playing with Polarity, Forgiveness, and Connecting with Hormones, detailed below.

### Daily Journal

- Check-in with your progress and understanding. Note any recent mental or emotional contractions, expansions, or questions.
- Reflect on any new experiences you have during exercises.
- Pay attention to your dreams. During this phase, your dreams can be a powerful way to restructure old patterns. Journal about any notable dreams as soon as you wake up. Sometimes, they can be difficult to analyze. You can use an online dream dictionary to help you analyze them. Sometimes, telling a friend about it can reveal new insights for you as well.

### Tools to Practice Throughout Your Daily Life

- Watching the Thinker
- Steps to Change a Pattern
- Movement
- Playing with Polarity*
- Forgiveness*
- Connect with the Felt Sense of Hormones*

*New practice

# Add to Your Daily Meditation: Sacral Chakra Humming

The sacral chakra includes themes of emotions and feelings. Life has a sense of flow when this chakra is clear and balanced. Pay attention to insights when patterns that have to do with the themes of this chakra come up. Don't engage with them to understand during meditation. Make a note of them in your journal after your practice.

Perform your everyday meditation by readying your space, creating safety and comfort, breathwork, humming, and completing your practice through the root chakra.

Now add the sacral chakra section while continuing to hum:

1. Move your awareness and energy from the root chakra to the sacral chakra. Notice how, as you bring the flames up, they surround the sacrum. The red fire begins to condense as it moves into the orange lava-like flow of the sacral chakra. Using your breath, feed the sacrum this fire. This chakra takes the powerful energy of the root to create through water. This is where fire meets water to make something new. Imagine the flow pulsating with energy as you hum. You can sense the energy and a feeling of vast, potent resources, like information coming together from within. The power of creation and destruction are here. This is the art of recreating yourself as you evolve throughout your life. You are being born over and over again within one lifetime as you create your new realities like an artist.

2. Take a deep breath and trust your inner power to create. Feel the depth and endlessness of what is possible here: the primordial soup that makes form. Here, all the emotions exist. Imagine feeling all the emotions within that come together to shape geometries, shapes, and colors. This is contained in the

womb space (whether male or female), where all your potentials exist.

3. As you feel the process come to completion, finish your practice as before. Keep your eyes closed and do a physical body scan with your hands, massaging and touching your body parts to ground yourself in the body and create comfort within. If you feel pulled, sit with your experience and see if anything arises.

Journal about anything impactful from your experience.

Below, we introduce your additional practices meant to be rotated in at the end of your daily meditation throughout month 2. You will start all meditations as you always have with the following: readying yourself, creating safety and comfort, breathwork, and watching the thinker.

Then, add one of the following practices to your meditation. Close the meditations as usual and journal about what arises.

## Playing with Polarity

Shifting your perspective to see the world through the lens of polarity as creation is one of the most life-changing shifts you can make. You will be amazed at how applying this understanding leads to deepened freedom, where fear and worry fade. The first step is to tell yourself to see everything happening for you and not to you. Then you also need to apply these concepts about polarity to your life to truly understand how it behaves in your world.

This will also help you better understand your experience and how reality works more fundamentally. The practice is simply seeing it everywhere because polarity exists on every level of our reality, from the human to the spiritual.

Now that you know you have been in the dance of polarity all your life, let's apply a method that helps to move emotions trapped in the body. The idea is not that these contracting emotions are bad. We are not meeting them from a place of wanting to escape them. This is how they get condensed and relegated to some part of your body in the first place. This practice will help you fully feel and integrate them.

Unintegrated emotions are  where density comes from. The unique technology of our bodies can help us process and integrate emotions in a relatively straightforward practice. When every cell and atom in your body connects with and understands the emotion, it suddenly integrates and shifts. This is one facet of the amazing technology that you are. Remember, the goal is not to escape the emotion but to integrate it through internal understanding, communication, and connection. Let's try it!

1. Lie down comfortably and clear your mind. Consider a past situation where you felt a specific contracting emotion. Initially, knowing why this emotion came up is essential. Ask yourself why you had that emotional reaction. What place of separation was it stimulating in you to bring it to your awareness?

2. Now, thank the situation and the persons involved for bringing this juicy place of separation to your awareness. Feel the gratitude in your heart space.

3. Then, the story of that situation can be let go of, leaving only the emotion. When you focus on the story, you are stuck in a limbic system loop and will remain there. Drop the story and find the emotion. It can be fear, anger, grief, shame, guilt, worry, jealousy, or something else.

4. Identify where that emotion is in the body. This can be challenging if you are not used to connecting with your body in subtle ways. However, this practice will help develop this

superpower. Common places for emotions are in the heart or gut. If you don't know where, simply make it up.

5. Imagine now that the emotion is a field. You can even imagine it as a puddle of emotion that you get down into. What color and texture does it have?

6. Next, invite this field into your body to meet every cell and every atom. Start with your feet. Invite the emotion in. See the color and texture of the emotion entering your feet. Tell yourself you are safe if this feels uncomfortable, and continue inviting it in. Throughout this process, remind yourself that you are safe and this is the way to self-integration.

7. The center of your cells acts as a technology of transmutation. When the emotion is acknowledged by every cell in your body, it will shift and change. Continue to bring the emotion up through the body until it reaches the top of your head.

8. You should notice a shift in the energy. Check back with the original area of your body to see if you can still find the emotion there. If you can, every cell has not let it in. Do the visualization again and pay attention to where it might get stuck. Check the back side of the body, heart, knees, and hips. These are common places that resist letting emotions in. Invite the emotion into that place specifically and tell yourself that you are safe to do this.

9. The last step is to feel gratitude and optimism in your heart: gratitude for the experiences that led you to this moment and the amazing potential that will meet you in future moments. This completes the circuit of poles.

Occasionally, this practice will make you feel heavy before the emotion shifts. If this happens, feel the heaviness for a few minutes until it moves. Sometimes, the original emotion shifts after this practice, and another becomes apparent. If this happens, repeat the practice with the new emotion.

This exercise was adapted from one introduced to me by a friend of mine, Dr. Cody Golman.

The more you practice these techniques, the more you will realize your power over your experience, access more freedom, and become open to the truth of who you are. Your next additional practice to alternate in your daily meditations is forgiveness.

## Forgiveness

You might think that you know how to forgive and decide to skip this section, but I advise against it. Doing so will only slow your progress. If you have a trigger reaction to this section, try to build awareness that this reaction is stimulating something for you—a juicy place of isolation waiting to be connected!

This is not always easy, but it will be some of the most freeing and vital work you will do. The truth is your capacity to forgive *directly* impacts your capacity for love. By releasing emotional density, you create more space in your heart.

Imagine the mountain of accumulated hurts that have gone unfor-given in life. This can bog you down with barriers of separation, both from those who have hurt you and others with whom you wish to have a deeper connection.

If doing this as part of your daily meditation, perform the first steps to set up your practice (readying yourself, creating safety and com-fort, breathwork, humming, and, at the end, closing your practice).

To help you, here are the three main facets of forgiveness:

## 1. Learn to See All Your Life Experiences as Happening for You, Not to You

Every difficult circumstance in your life has been an opportunity for growth. Opportunities not taken turn into bigger and bigger mountains trying to get your attention. The truth is, before you were incarnated, you chose these lessons for your soul's growth. The thorny, difficult places will return until you figure them out. With this perspective, you can start to see the difficult people in your life as your greatest helpers. Maybe you will not be best friends with them during your physical life, but in the spiritual realm, they are some of your greatest allies and partners.

## 2. Realize That Any Person That You Forgive Is Not Freed from Blame or Given an Out—You Are Freeing Yourself

This is where people get stuck—they feel like their grudge toward another is punishing that person. Again, it is not. That person is likely unaware of how you feel or that they did anything wrong. This brings us to another important factor: you need not talk to someone directly to forgive them and free yourself.

It can all be done energetically within your body and mind. What are you freeing yourself from exactly? You are freeing yourself from the limbic system loop that keeps you stuck and negatively affects your physiology, limiting the experience of an expanded you.

## 3. Seek the Lesson That Your Soul Wants to Learn through Your Human Life

This is the practice of seeing from a higher perspective and integrating the learning. It is possible for this all to happen once you have initiated true forgiveness for the other person. However, you may also need to sift through the situation to find the lesson consciously. Here are a few questions that may help:

- How has this situation made you a better or stronger person?
- Did this situation show you where you needed to voice your boundaries or what you wanted better?
- How else might this situation have helped you grow or understand yourself?

## Connect with the Felt Sense of Hormones

With our liberating previous practices, you may find that connecting with your felt sense of hormones has changed or become easier. If practicing this as a part of your daily meditation, include the preparation steps (readying yourself, creating safety, breathwork, and comfort, humming, and at the end closing your practice).

Then do the practice of connecting with each hormone (dopamine, oxytocin, serotonin, etc.) as described in the previous chapter. Think of times that remind you of those feelings and descriptions. What is the story? Use as many of your senses as you can to remember and connect that to a feeling of health and vitality in the body. Reexperience it now! Journal about any insights.

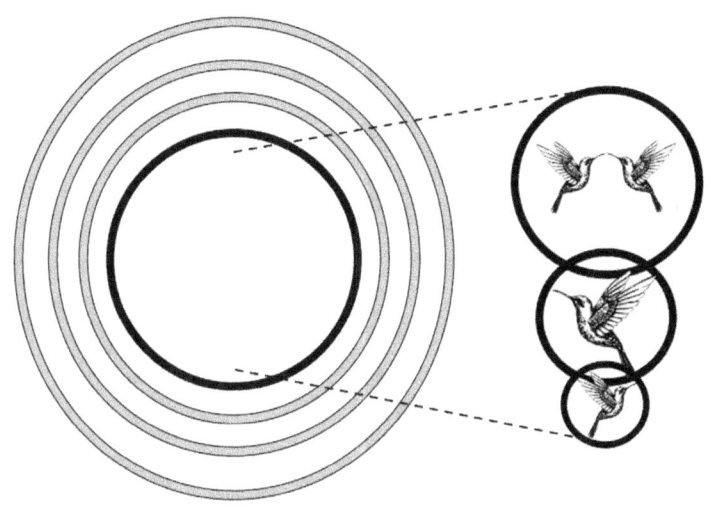

# Third Octave:
# Chapters 5 and 6

## Freeing the Mind (Physical Plane)

You are so much more than your thoughts. You are so much more than slow and unconscious evolution. When you free your mind, you free your emotions, and open more deeply to yourself.

***Old Perspective:*** *An unconscious directive of "I am a limited individual human."*

***New Perspective:*** *A conscious mental engagement, as in "I am a spiritual being having a human experience."*

# The Evolution of the Brain, Separation, and You

*The measure of intelligence is the ability to change.*

—Albert Einstein

Love is the union of both sides of the brain. Love is the awareness of being.

This chapter will continue our discussion of behavior and the mind and how your consciousness contributes to your experience. We will also examine how lacking presence in the moment contributes to anxiety and explore the relationship of our brain to emotions. Further, we will focus on how the nervous system relates to physiology and creates our mental experience through thought.

The secret is that you have more control of these systems than you may realize. This is the importance of utilizing the consciousness that you already have.

## Why So Much Separation If There Are All These "Connecting" Hormones?

*Homo sapiens* is a Latin term that means "knowing" or "wise man." Over millions of years, our cognition has evolved, reaching heights we couldn't have imagined. Humans have subsequently achieved incredible feats with technology, ultimately transforming every facet of life. Now, consider how far humanity has come in just the past four decades. Most people in the early 1980s would not believe what computers can currently do, let alone cell phones and the internet!

And what about our ancestors one hundred, one thousand, or even one million years ago? They would not even be able to conceive of the technology currently in use, for they had absolutely no context for any of it. During this time, humans have continually honed and specialized their cognitive skills through the evolution of the brain. However, these changes expanded to support left-brain ways of engaging with the world.

> *This all started when consciousness evolved to the point that it could begin to have self-awareness and a separate experience.*

Every evolution can have a perceived positive and a negative aspect; there will always be polarity. The development of self-awareness has allowed humans to expand and create in incredible ways. However, it is also what led to our experience of isolation and disconnection. In this case, the poles are the positive (the evolution) and the negative (the factor that can become out of balance). It is still all creation.

This is exemplified in the story of Adam and Eve and their eating of the apple of knowledge, representing a step of human ascension toward knowledge. The knowledge acquired was specifically self-awareness and allowed humans to have consciousness through the creation of the ego. The ego then generated an artificial sense of self and a singular experience based on external things, history, and mental-emotional experiences while remaining separate from others, the universe, and God.

*The unintegrated ego flourishes amid resistance, control, power, defense, and attack. The brain has evolved to create an object-referral perspective in which only the self is identified with the experience it is having.*

The ego, which often rules the person and is their source of identity, is connected with the brain's left hemisphere. An illustration of this relationship is exemplified in the personal story of neuroscientist Jill Taylor. After having a stroke in the left side of her brain, Taylor was astounded to realize that she no longer experienced feelings of jealousy or the tendency to be arrogant or sarcastic.

It was not until the left hemisphere came back "online" that, to her dismay, those personality traits reappeared. The point is not to vilify the ego but to remember that this part of the personality is not who you are. It is simply an evolution of the brain to create a sense of identity and to keep you safe. The goal is to understand the rightful place of the ego, especially in our current evolution in consciousness. But for now, let's delve deeper into how the ego develops.

Newborn infants are without an ego for some time, existing in an unconscious state of unity and complete connection with all, where they operate and process the world from the right side of their brain. The ego begins to develop after children learn to speak, at which point they increasingly identify with their name and the ideas of *me* and *mine*. Then further explorations of social interactions reinforce it.

These developments also correlate with an upsurge in accessing the left side of the brain, which fully comes to fruition around puberty. When the child then goes to school, they continuously and often unconsciously absorb more and more from the external world. By the time the child is older, they fully identify with their name and personal and learned stories. This increasing content of the ego creates a mask of who they think they are.

Complete identification with the false self or unbalanced ego can create suffering and friction during human life and often shows up as a them-versus-me mentality. This is duality consciousness, and many people dwell in this state. It is the cornerstone of all human conflict, whether person-to-person contention or warring countries. Living from the unbalance ego and left brain keeps you constantly in either future thinking, which creates anxiety about things that will likely not happen, or past thinking, where you are reliving difficult experiences.

The first step in cultivating this awareness is realizing that there is only *ever* the present moment. Many physicists agree that the ideas of the past and future don't exist. Einstein called time a "stubbornly persistent illusion." It turns out that time is not a fundamental quantity in the big picture of reality. It is relative to the observer, meaning there is no absolute time. If absolute time existed, it would mean that time would be the same for all observers. In physics, you can choose a specific reference system for this to be true, but there is no universal time across all space.

Think about your individual perception of how time passes. You may have noticed that this seems to shift based on your activity. If you are doing something difficult, time may go by slowly, whereas if you enjoy yourself, it seems to fly by. In both situations, the clock is ticking at the same pace.

Perception of time is based on the experience of the observer. Different brain states and hormones can shift your sense of how fast or slow time is passing. Being present in the moment is often a way to slow down this perception. When your being is in an excited state, stimulating the nervous system, time may pass more slowly or quickly depending. When the body is in an energy-conservation mode (less awareness, less presence), time can seem to pass more quickly.

*The presence described here is an awareness of what you are doing, thinking, and feeling. To be present is to feel that you are. This is related to the total presence that is available in deep meditation. When you go into the deepest recesses of who you are, you find your I AM presence projecting itself to create you/itself in human form.*

Another way to look at the passage of time is through the lens of expansion and contraction. When you are expanding, time may seem to move more slowly. For example, when you are more present in the moment, you expand your awareness in the now, and your perception of time slows. Expansion of awareness slows time. On the other hand, contraction of awareness speeds up the experience of time. Anyone who has spent a day worrying (a contraction) about something that has not yet happened has experienced this.

Although it is healthy to engage with future thinking to plan for our lives, it's important to avoid remaining there for too long—or else you miss out on actually living! Similarly, it can be useful to dip into the past to reflect and integrate wisdom, but living from the past only creates suffering.

We came to experience the here and now as humans. In chapter 1, we explored the brain's ability to engage in future thinking for things like pair bonding. Now, we will apply this to every level of our experience, from individual goals to future planning for society and the world. It has been part of our evolution, although it has also become easily unregulated, leading to imbalance.

*This leads to seeking outside yourself to find clues or to be told who you are. Being present becomes difficult here as you can't hold your center.*

The inability to be present at times will naturally happen because of the brain's capabilities; it only becomes a problem when you spend the bulk of your time there. If you find yourself living in the mind-set of, *I need to attain* [fill in the blank] *to be happy*, you are spending your time in the future.

Have you ever reached a big goal you had been working toward for a long time, only to find emptiness at the end? This is because the roller coaster of getting there was the fulfilling part, as that created your growth. Attaining the goal signifies the dawn of a new phase.

> *Being stuck in anxious thinking of the future or reliving past stories are symptoms of separation from yourself, others, and the broader universe.*

You believe you are merely your thoughts when you solely identify with your mind. Then, thinking manages to become the problem that pulls you out of the present moment. Even in the present, you can watch as the mind tries to pull you into past or future thinking. The magic lies beyond the thinking mind in a higher level of consciousness that includes intuition, love, and compassion.

> *Our level of consciousness is an important driver of the quality of our experience. This awareness is the first step in evolving your consciousness.*

Most people operate from hectic minds that plague them throughout their days and even keep them up at night. How good can the quality of your life be when you are anxious and can't sleep? Unconsciousness may make time seemingly pass quickly, overwhelming you and activating nervous system states, like fight or flight.

Discipline is then needed to teach the mind that there are more tools and higher levels you can access. Being present in the moment and understanding the mind for what it is—a tool that helps humans process sensory information— and then choosing how to respond *consciously*. It's also important to acknowledge that you are both the human and the spirit in this particular play.

Without this discipline, you are susceptible to responding to the outside world from reflex or being triggered by specific events or emotions. The issues arise when there is a heavy reliance on the tool of our ego, like a crutch that makes us feel safe but also limits us. This is an example of confusing the unbalanced ego with who you truly are.

Around 90 percent of our thoughts occur automatically. This automation drives our behavioral patterns. Your brain constantly assesses your environment, looking for potential threats and opportunities. This dynamic comes from an evolution of our brains and quantifies our instincts.

These subconscious behaviors may even have become so ingrained that we don't know why we do them. When you become the watcher of your thoughts, you shift from the left side of your brain to the right side, even changing the frequency of the current running through your brain. This shifts your experience and opens awareness to existing opportunities, previously unnoticed.

All that truly matters surfaces from this access to higher consciousness. This is how the current evolution begins within each individual—it's the budding of your conscious control over the brain. It creates new patterns of stimulation and leads to an increase in positive hormone circulation.

## Evolution of the Brain

To better understand the journey ahead, let's consider previous stages of the brain's evolution. There are three different brains, the second and third of which evolved on top of the first. Each correlates with a giant evolutionary leap. The initial brain is called the reptilian brain and covers the survival impulses we have in common with fish and reptiles.

The reptilian brain (sometimes called the lizard brain) includes the spinal cord and brainstem, which are responsible for autonomic functions that keep us alive, such as breathing or the beating of your heart. It also controls survival reflexes like activating fight, flight, fawn, or freeze responses.

Our brain comes preprogrammed with each of the four Fs to utilize as a distress response or to assess threats. A fight reaction to a situation would be to stay and face it and have a verbal or physical confrontation. Flight is when you run to escape when you feel threatened.

Freeze is similar to what opossums do: they activate such terror that they cannot move in emergent situations. The last of the four Fs, fawning, is often called the please-and-appease response to difficult situations. We all have a go-to F. Do you know what yours is? Knowing how you respond to challenging situations gives you information on your ingrained and unconscious patterns that may need rewiring.

It is thought that 150 million years ago, the limbic system began to evolve and finally appeared in small mammals. For the first time, the brain was able to record agreeable and disagreeable experiences and store them in memory. For humans, this system is also the source of emotions. To that point, have you ever wondered what the purpose of having emotions is? There is the human perspective and the broader spiritual perspective.

Emotions are drivers of our experience and generate the impetus for all that we do. In the greater perspective, human emotions create energy for the universe. The endocrine system creates hormones that drive behaviors and generate energy through the chakra system. If your human emotions are creating energy with frequencies that permeate the planet and universe, what frequency are you contributing to the whole?

The limbic system includes the amygdala, hippocampus, hypothalamus, and pituitary gland. The hypothalamus secretes oxytocin, which is then stored in the pituitary gland. When signaled by the hypothalamus, the pituitary gland releases the oxytocin. The hypothalamus also makes vasopressin, a hormone that regulates water and sodium levels.

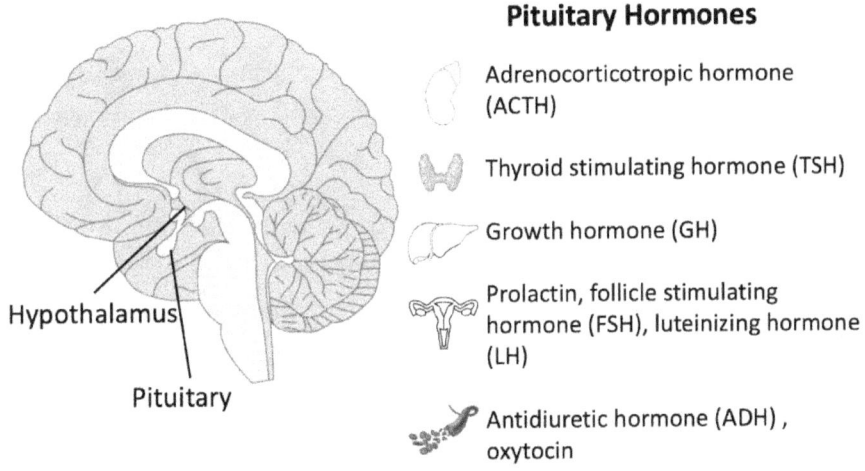

**Pituitary Hormones**

Adrenocorticotropic hormone (ACTH)

Thyroid stimulating hormone (TSH)

Growth hormone (GH)

Prolactin, follicle stimulating hormone (FSH), luteinizing hormone (LH)

Antidiuretic hormone (ADH) , oxytocin

Hypothalamus

Pituitary

The pituitary gland makes additional important hormones:

- *Adrenocorticotropic hormone* (ATCH) stimulates the adrenal gland to secrete stress hormones.
- *Follicle-stimulating hormone* stimulates sperm production in men and estrogen and egg development in women.
- *Growth hormone* stimulates growth in children and aids in maintaining healthy muscle and bone levels in adults.
- *Luteinizing hormone* stimulates ovulation in women and testosterone in men.

- *Prolactin* incites the production of breast milk.
- *Thyroid-stimulating hormone*, as the name suggests, stimulates the production of thyroid hormones, leading to primary metabolism and nervous system support.

You may notice that many of these hormones oversee mammalian behavior. The limbic system is often called the "paleo" or "old" mammal brain. The general function of this area is to create hormones that lead to emotions, social hierarchy, and other purposes specific to mammals.

*This is the same technology you are using for spiritual expansions in your meditations with the activations of glands and the subsequent opening of your chakras.*

You may wonder: Do nonmammals like reptiles and fish have oxytocin hormones? As it turns out, some fish with a rudimentary thalamus also have a hormonal version of oxytocin called isotocin. Birds and reptiles even have their own version, mesotocin.

Whatever name it is given, this hormone makes these creatures more apt to approach one another, helps them size up an opponent for conflict, and can even make them act more submissively when challenged. These molecules are the ancient origins of mammals' oxytocin.

Their existence supports the observation that changes in endocrine function likely underlie behavioral evolution.

The hypothalamus links the nervous system to the body's hormone system, the endocrine system, via the pituitary gland. This means it is the place where emotions drive behaviors. This is also exactly where the next conscious evolution described in this book begins.

First, you must cultivate felt senses of forgiveness and gratitude and begin to heal your unbalanced feelings of separation on multiple levels. This will lead you to higher states of Love.

For this reason, the following chapter's expansion practices will help you learn a new way of being for your hypothalamus and pituitary gland through the experience of higher emotions. This will not only help change your behaviors but also help you evolve your mind and life to surpass the limitations of the mammalian brain.

The neocortex is the most recent evolutionary addition to the brain. This is considered part of the brain and comprises about 76 percent of the brain's total tissue volume. Much of our recent neurological evolution has been geared toward developing this area of the brain.

The neocortex controls things like spatial perception and reasoning, conscious thought, complex memory processing, long-term memory, the transmission of sensory information, short-term memory, higher social and emotional processing, avoidant conditioning, and sleep and learning processing.

Humans have three interconnected parts of the brain that evolved over long periods to be the sources of survival (reptilian), feeling (limbic), and thinking (neocortex). You would think that the higher-functioning neocortex would always control the older parts of the brain; however, both reptilian and limbic systems can commandeer processing power. When this happens, your focus and drive completely shift, deeply affecting your human experience.

When these other brain areas take over, it usually is due to stress or fear. For example, if your reptilian brain has taken over, you are likely operating from scarcity and lack of safety. Moreover, this part of your brain can control food choices, so you may crave sugar and carbohydrates to create safety when operating from it.

If the limbic system is front and center, you could be caught in what is known as a limbic system loop. This stress cycle impairs digestion, immunity, memory, and mood and is linked to previous emotional experiences. Post-traumatic stress disorder, for example, is a common limbic system issue. This happens when memories and experiences are not properly processed, and their related emotions are not expressed.

*If you are in a state of stress and fear, you cannot experience states of connectedness and love.*

Now we understand how the brain evolved its three main vertical sections. The next perspective to consider is the workings of the left and right hemispheres and how they play into our human experience, helping us understand future evolutions of our brains.

## Right and Left Hemispheres of the Brain

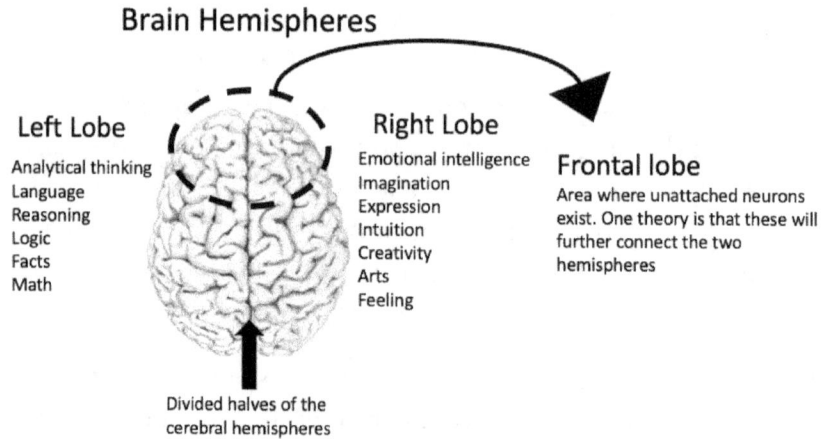

**Brain Hemispheres**

**Left Lobe**

Analytical thinking
Language
Reasoning
Logic
Facts
Math

**Right Lobe**

Emotional intelligence
Imagination
Expression
Intuition
Creativity
Arts
Feeling

**Frontal lobe**

Area where unattached neurons exist. One theory is that these will further connect the two hemispheres

Divided halves of the cerebral hemispheres

As mentioned, the brain is divided into left and right sides or hemispheres. The left hemisphere is where logic, analysis, and language occur, as well as organizational, sequential, and deliberate thinking.

The right hemisphere is more intuitive, empathetic, and spontaneous. It comes from more of a holistic and integrative perspective.

A young structure in the brain connects both hemispheres called the corpus callosum. This is the great integrator of things like motor function and thought. Thinking in terms of language is done chiefly in the left hemisphere, and the right hemisphere "thinks" more in terms of pictures, sensations, and feelings. The corpus callosum allows both to co-occur so that you can communicate or listen, creating sensations from the right brain.

Engaging in your next evolution means consciously knowing what part of the brain you are operating from and using that awareness to choose and activate your frontal lobe. This occurs by experiencing higher emotions and the subsequent release of hormones throughout the body. Each time you do this, you create new neural pathways that support continued access to these higher-brain and physiological functions.

This can be experienced most commonly through language, which can evoke emotions. Have you ever read a poem that made you feel an emotion like reverence, awe, or even Love? When you read the words, they are first understood in the left side of the brain, creating an emotion in the right side. This can also happen when you speak words of depth or vulnerability and you experience a deep feeling. These situations use both hemispheres of the brain and result in hormonal release.

When and where does consciousness come in? If you ask Dr. Peter Fenwick, a neuropsychologist who has studied end-of-life phenomena, it's not inside the brain! Based on his observations, Fenwick believes the brain filters consciousness and it exists in omnipresence as a basic property of the universe, just like light, electrons, or black holes.

*Furthermore, Fenwick believes that our consciousness tricks us into believing that we are in a false reality separate from everything else, yet we are all connected in truth.*

While our brains are the filter of consciousness, it is impossible to perceive this truth or the whole of reality fully. This creates an illusion of separation. In Fenwick's theory, only upon death can you fully experience the oneness from which you came. However, I believe that oneness becomes more accessible through cultivating your right brain and further alignments on your spiritual journey.

If you think about it, it's not hard to believe that the brain allows us to feel separate. The awareness that you are more than your mind and body is the doorway to the beginning of conscious expansion. Let's contemplate why this can initially be difficult to perceive and, therefore, believe.

## Human Visible Electromagnetic Spectrum

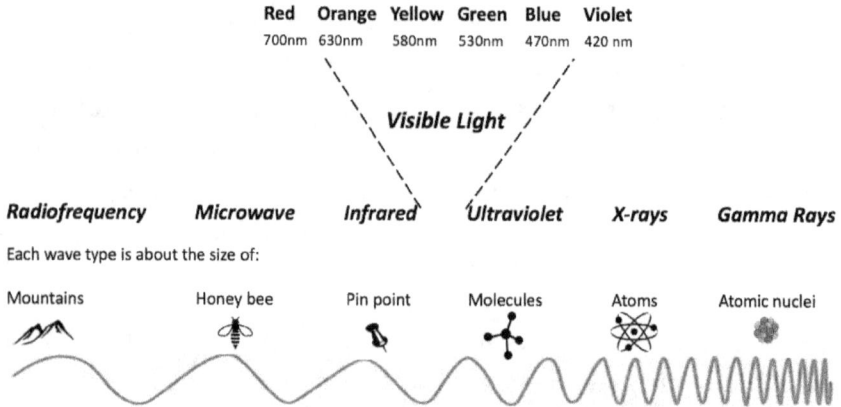

Consider our vision, for example. Our brain has evolved to see a range of the electromagnetic spectrum, yet seeing radio waves or x-rays is not possible. This is how the human brain evolved to perceive reality only for survival. Birds, however, perceive the ultraviolet part of the light spectrum as part of their evolution.

Humans have a brain that is a product of evolution, creating the reality you *think* you live in. What you perceive as green doesn't exist as that color; it depends on whose brain you perceive it through. You perceive a specific frequency of light that your brain processes as green.

Remember that the brain is a sensing and perceiving organ with a main purpose of making decisions with information-perceptions to keep you alive. These perceptions are limited to the five senses—sight, smell, taste, hearing, and touch. It is the same for consciousness being filtered by the brain: we think what we perceive is the whole truth, but it is merely a glimpse of it!

This is why science has difficulty studying what is beyond the "normal" five senses, and exploring these areas is often referred to as pseudoscience or "spiritual." My point is that these additional senses are still part of the natural world and, therefore, are also essential to scientific exploration, even if scientists do not yet know how to utilize, qualify, or quantify them.

That said, quantum physics research is assembling observations that approach some of what people in the spiritual realm report. Although this falls beyond the scope of our exploration, there are many publications that touch on how these concepts relate.

A few of these articles are:

- "The Creation of Matter from Light" from the Brookhaven National Laboratory particle collider
- "Mental States Follow Quantum Mechanics During Perception and Cognition" by Elio Conte et al.

- "Demonstration of Quantum Energy Teleportation on Super-conducting Quantum Hardware" by Kazuki Ikeda
- "John Wheeler's Participatory Universe" in *Futurism* by Marina Jones

Next, we dive deeper into themes of perception and consciousness to further illuminate how our individual experience relates to spiritual evolution and Love.

## Perception

Perception is the cumulation of your brain using your five senses and intuition to understand your surroundings and reality. This perception is based on the individual's experience, a point that is well depicted in the above cartoon. Further, perception is also affected by the level of consciousness of the person perceiving and the breadth of perspectives they can hold.

## Exploring the Nature of Consciousness

Let's bring our attention back to consciousness for a moment. For animals, the psychological litmus test for basic conscious awareness is to know the self from the other. This means the animal has awareness that it is a separate creature from others.

For this reason, most species on the planet are not considered conscious. Generally speaking, only humans and great apes have passed the standard mirror test, which, as the name suggests, is used to determine whether or not subjects can recognize themselves in a mirror. However, there have been individual elephants, dolphins, a Eurasian magpie, and even a few ants that have passed.

We are not alone in the most basic ways of being conscious animals. What makes humans different is our ability to be aware of that awareness. As described by Erik Hoffmann in his book *New Brain, New World*, this occurs when the left hemisphere is aware of the right and vice versa. This aligns with Buddhist perspectives and, more recently, Eckhardt Tolle.

## Consciousness and the Brain

Evidence suggests the corpus callosum is not currently fully activated, as it is a relatively new development of the cortex. Inside it is a bundle of unattached neurons. Hoffman believes these unattached neurons in the corpus callosum are not yet mature enough for communication.

He states that the neurons here are likely part of a future evolution that will bring us to higher consciousness by providing increased connectivity between hemispheres. My theory is that deeper activations of heart intelligence through the experience of higher emotions catalyze neural growth between hemispheres. This is the evolution that we are collectively working toward. When more people have access to increased neural connections, wholeness in the experience of Love will grow.

The right side is where consciousness first inhabits the brain and is mainly seated until you are about two years old. Then, as language evolves, the left side becomes the primary seat of consciousness. Some, like Harvard psychologist Julian Jaynes, believe that the left hemisphere evolved after the right side. The fact that the right hemisphere develops much sooner in the human fetus supports this theory. This may mean that early humans mostly lived from the right side of their brains before language.

Once one understands how the brain evolved and what the purpose of that evolution was, the pieces of a puzzle begin to emerge. This illuminates how our human experience can be affected by the level of consciousness we are operating from. As mentioned before, our consciousness can be "in" the reptilian survival part of the brain, the limbic system or emotional part, or the most evolved thinking part of the brain, the neocortex.

> *However, what is opening as a new evolution is an expansion to reutilize the right side of the brain and the intelligence of the heart to reach new levels of human experience.*

Brain evolution during the reptilian era happened very slowly and unconsciously. The term *unconscious* here relates to the lack of any use of consciousness, unlike the active subconscious, when there is a deeper drive beneath a behavior. Subsequent evolution during the limbic phase was partially driven by changes in the endocrine system that modified behavior and was still primarily unconscious. Next, there was a time of advancements in thinking with the neocortex, which opened the potential for conscious access to evolution using the limbic system.

The model described here is a spiral path that loops back to repurposing and reintegrating the right side of the brain. Evolution often utilizes already established machinery like this, as you saw in chapter

1. Your machinery is primed. Now, it will take your awareness, perspective, and dedication to make the shifts ahead.

## Is It Easy to Change the Brain's Patterns?

The short answer is that it depends. The ability to create flexibility in how you relate to the world depends on your personality, age, experiences, and the level of safety your nervous system feels. While it may be easier for one person over another, it is possible for everyone.

Metamorphic fields, introduced earlier, also have a role in the ease individuals experience. This is because these fields underpin normal evolution and often longer time scales. In this journey, you're consciously making different choices to change your mind and how your physiology works to accelerate your personal evolution.

Remember, metamorphic fields are a driver of physical creation, so your previous states and perceived experiences most impact you. The evolution will be slower if these previous states have a slower vibration. These are the fields with which you resonate and continually inform your current field. You can think of these as your habits.

Just as in Newton's Law of Motion ("a body in motion stays in motion"), you will continue to do what you have done in the past if your unconscious habits lead your mind. This is evolution without consciousness and can be what keeps us on a more slowly evolving path. We can evolve more quickly when the field is engaged and worked with consciously.

*This is why you are employing higher frequency emotional states for conscious evolution.*

Alternatively, without conscious engagement to change, habits and patterns persist. This is when something might come in to jolt us out of this resonance with the self. It may occur in the form of an accident, illness, divorce, loss of a job, or other difficulties that shift your state and offer an opportunity for change. This doesn't just happen on the individual level but the collective as well. War, sickness, and other global difficulties bring the opportunity to create change for masses of people.

This has certainly been my experience. I have been in multiple car accidents over my lifetime. Although the cities they occurred in were different, the circumstances were similar. I was at a stop at each one, and the car behind me hit me. From a third-dimensional perspective, none were my fault; something else was behind their occurrence.

In each successive accident, the person hitting me went faster than the last. It took me five car accidents to finally get the message: I was the one who needed to slow down and listen to messages I had been ignoring. Sometimes, tuning in and listening to your inner guidance *is* the conscious engagement needed. However, this is not something our society makes time for or venerates.

Each accident created space in my life for self-care like physical and massage therapy. The last accident left me with a concussion that led to post-concussion syndrome, and it took me almost two years to get back to normal. That one was particularly debilitating, and I was strongly encouraged by my doctor to take three months off.

Even though I struggled through daily activities at this point, I was crushed to hear that I should avoid work—and for months, at that! That thought pattern is all the evidence you need to know that my mind was stuck on a limited path.

At the same time, I had been asking for more from my life and the universe. The misstep was that I asked but did not listen for guidance. This is why such a large force (or crash) had to enter my life. Before, I was unwilling or too afraid to make big changes.

Each of these accidents led to some of the most beautiful break-throughs, personal growth, and advancements in every area of life—including my writing of this book. I'm not telling you that it was easy because it has been a transformation that has taken effort on many fronts.

Something in me shifted that allowed me to see and take opportuni-ties when they aligned with what I wanted to create in my life. Then ease did come in, not in the sense that I won a million dollars, and now I don't have to worry, but more so, I am securely on my path and know that all I am experiencing is in alignment.

Regarding metamorphic fields, Dr. Sheldrake talks about a new field's origin as a "creative jump or synthesis," which can also be defined as a quantum leap. While we don't need to wait for a difficult life cir-cumstance to bring this on, you need a strong desire for expansion or evolution and find tools to help you reach it.

Untangling mental constructs is what the following sections explore. This occurs through perspective shifts alongside tools to help release the mental density that may be holding you back. Then something amazing happens: you have greater access to states of gratitude, awe, forgiveness, and admiration.

This allows you to see and take opportunities as they arise and access deeper authentic parts of yourself, leading to Love. Then, you enter the driver's seat of your life rather than letting your old patterns affect your perception of reality. This will be an essential foundation for further chapters.

## How to Balance Your Separate Self (Ego)

Previously, the ego has been discussed as the creator of our sense of identity and all your feelings of separation.

*As we move more into psychological principles, I would like to substitute the term* separate self *for ego.*

This is the only substitution I make in this book. I do so here because many of our words have acquired the baggage of our culture through years of overuse. Once that happens, they lose their purity of meaning, and it becomes easy to be triggered by them. In this instance, ego defines an evolution of the brain that has acquired a bad reputation in our culture.

When it's understood that ego helps create the illusion of our separateness, it can be seen as a tool for our further development. We rename the ego as the separate self, which reminds us of this connection.

*As part of the human condition, we get an individual experience with a unique personality. This is possible solely due to the separate self. It is only when it is out of balance that it creates suffering. A loss of balance occurs when you seek outside yourself and forget you are the center of your experience.*

There is polarity implied in the new term *separate self:* either you are balanced in your experience, or your separation creates an unbalanced need for external acceptance or validation. However, the truth is that it all exists inside you in every moment, waiting for you to become aware of yourself.

The ability to process human experiences varies from person to person, depending on how one's nervous system is wired and the strength of the imbalance of the separate self. We have all seen it happen: two people can react differently to the same situation based on past programming. One may not even have a nervous system response to specific stimulation, while another could have a deeply jarring response that causes emotional dysregulation for days, weeks, or longer.

For example, have you witnessed another driver get cut off in traffic and lose their cool? They might zoom by the other person, yelling profanities and honking their horn, indicating that they were triggered and felt disrespected by the other person's actions. Another person might have a different reaction to the same situation.

Most people have experienced being cut off in traffic, and different responses are possible. Maybe you felt offended by the stranger's lack of consideration, and it took a few minutes to shake off that feeling. Or perhaps it didn't faze you, and you told yourself that the person must have been late for something important. In this way we each live in a different reality, and our reactions are a guidance system for the type we have created for ourselves.

Often, people who are stuck reliving their past have reactions that are primed by multiple previous situations. This happens because of a limbic system loop, as discussed earlier. Wherein difficult experiences have not been processed and integrated, which is tough to do when the separate self remembers them. I see this as an evolutionary mechanism that serves as a reminder not to repeat a past disagreeable experience.

*An unbalanced separate self acts mainly as an unconscious warning system that can be hypersensitized or confused about the signals it receives.*

It's like there is an initial unconscious reflex then transmitted to a loud conscious voice in our heads to take an action that keeps us safe. One of the defining characteristics of this voice is that it has a negative perspective, pointing out fears, insecurities, and doubts. Another telltale sign that the separate self (imbalanced) is active is that you believe you are either better than or inferior to someone else.

Triggers and other contracting messages from the separate self have led to much isolation and human suffering. This was the impetus for the development of psychotherapy. Most are familiar with Sigmund Freud, the Austrian neurologist who founded psychoanalysis in the late nineteenth century. Freud mapped the stages of human development and posited that unconscious memories, thoughts, and urges influence behavior.

Talk therapy is based on the concept that talking about your problems can help relieve them and is considered one of Freud's greatest contributions to psychology. However, while many have experienced some benefit, it has also remained ultimately ineffective. It's clear we still need a better management tool to understand and integrate messages from the separate self and expand into more of our True Selves.

This takes an earnest awareness of the contracting emotion, why that response occurred, and an engagement with higher emotions. Then, you can transcend identification with merely the separate self, and maturation can occur, giving you access to even higher levels of the self.

Enter Stuart Sovatsky, Ph.D., an incredibly accomplished Kundalini master and therapist with over fifty years of clinical experience. Sovatsky has written books like *Advanced Spiritual Intimacy* and many peer-reviewed articles on tantra, Kundalini, and how to create life-long love partnerships.

His views on Freud, fueled by his clinical observations, are quite provocative, and his perspective offers a lot of important information to our exploration of Love and its role in our evolution. Sovatsky contends that Freud-based psychology models, when used alone, move individuals away from Love rather than toward it, which creates unneeded distress in families and individuals.

Dr. Sovatsky also views Western psychology as developed by nine-teenth-century medical doctors looking from the perspective of what is "wrong" with a person. As such, they looked for common threads and found the problems began in childhood. However, when you focus on early life as the cause of all your problems, you diminish yourself, your connections, and your experiences.

Sovatsky also takes issue with the current psychological model, which suggests a need to "let go of" or "sit in" our emotions, includ-ing anger and hurt. He holds that these methods have proven not to work very well and have, instead, ruined countless marriages.

No one is suggesting that having these emotions is the problem. Instead, it is the lack of affection (e.g., compliments) and heartfelt appreciation shared by partners, the tendency not to be present with one another, and the inability to notice one's happiness with the other person. The current model only creates more distance between individuals—that is, separation. According to Sovatsky, this is a pri-mary contributing factor to the nearly 50 percent divorce rate in the United States.

Sovatsky also looks at the language used to describe difficult situa-tions humans experience during their lifetimes, including terms like *trauma* and *shell shock*. These are the linguistics of a combat zone, which only further impedes the healing process because it places peo-ple in a victim mode.

After decades of working with couples, Stovatsky has concluded that once there is love, you can find it again through the power of admira-tion. Admiration is the bridge to connection when it has been lost. This isn't a one-session practice; it often takes time to rebuild the connec-tion. However, the process is not difficult, and new patterns emerge.

This practice isn't just for partners but can be used with friends or anyone in your orbit. It consists of making eye contact, thanking people, admiring people, giving compliments, and noticing all the things in their life that you admire, including the memories you share. This will change your experience of the world, as it increases the love and connection hormones that circulate in your body and the person you are interacting with. It creates hope and excitement for each day.

This can also be a practice when difficult situations arise with others. When a friend, partner, relative, or even an acquaintance brings up a problem, thank them for bringing it up. The other person might then say, "You are welcome, and thank you for noticing and appreciating the problem." This balanced reception sets the tone for good communication and the co-creation of positive feelings.

Through admiration, you can stop defensive responses in yourself and others. It is essential to discuss the problem slowly. Then, as you speak to each other, use eye contact to let the other person know you hear them and care about their response. You might even thank them for their eye contact to let them know that you see they are trying and hearing you.

Letting them know they are being heard will, in turn, be appreciated. If they do not say they understand it in return, ask them how letting them know they are being listened to makes them feel. This is Sovatsky's method to stop triggering events where one or both feel they are not being heard.

The deeper parts of you, your soul and psyche, contain an endless supply of optimism. This occurs through faith, possibility, love, hope, and the like. You can use your separate self to focus on things in your life that are contractions (or growth opportunities) but return to your optimism and your soul. The more we return to this place, the more our lives align with our true nature so even deeper awareness can grow.

By practicing these admiration-based methods, Sovatsky has saved many marriages and resolved many conflicts. However, this only scratches the surface, so if you want to learn more about his process, check out Dr. Sovatsky's book *Words from the Soul.*

## The Trap of Victimhood

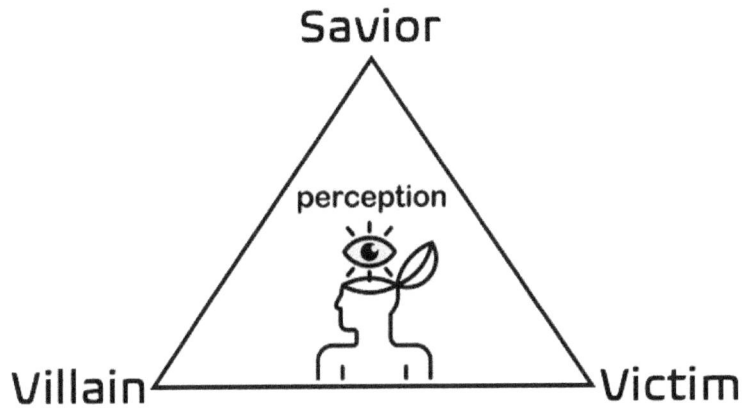

Stephen B. Karpman originally proposed the Karpman drama triangle to understand conflict in human interaction. This model includes the roles of Victim, Villain, and Savior (called initially the Victor). Notice this is another triangle diagram! This is another opportune application of polarity and creation. This time, it's between people.

In Dr. Sovatsky's view, the practice of admiration is enough to heal all between people, and he is right. However, understanding the drama triangle's inner workings can help bring awareness to potential triangles in life, including those where you have previously been stuck. Suppose you can access an understanding and application of the concepts of polarity and let others have their own experience. This scaffold brings greater understanding during the initial stages of shifting perspectives about interpersonal conflicts.

By being mindful of the dynamics described below, you can practice appreciation and forgiveness as balms that heal it all. Sometimes, this can open you up more deeply to the practice of admiration. Further, notice that feelings of separation held by each individual involved in the drama triangle hold it together.

Here is a description of the part each role plays to hold a drama triangle together:

- *The Victim.* This represents someone who is feeling or acting like a victim in a situation (not an actual victim). They may seek to convince others and themselves that they are powerless. They may be convinced that nothing can be done even if they try. The separate self uses this position as a defense. The Victim avoids change and lacks awareness of their true feelings.

   Taking a Victim mentality can lead a person to believe that they are doing everything to escape only to remain stuck in some way. The person in this role experiences feelings of oppression, helplessness, powerlessness, and shame. They seem unable to make decisions or receive insight.

   The Victim perpetuates the dynamic with the Villain. If the Villain leaves the situation, the Victim will subconsciously find someone else to fill that role. They will also seek help and create one or more Saviors to rescue them from the situation. When Saviors enter the triangle, they will often be recast in the Villain position at some point, and the situation will remain unchanged.

- *The Savior (Rescuer or Victor).* This role is of the enabler. Their intentions are often to genuinely aid in the situation, though the impetus for helping is often guilt. This guilt can easily turn to anger when their assistance does not generate the expected change. It is at this point that they become the Villain.

People who are chronic Saviors tend to put energy into other's drama as a way to ignore their own anxiety. The energy of their avoidance is then funneled into concern for the needs of the Victim.

* *The Villain (Persecutor)*. The person in this role insists that everything is the Victim's fault. The Villain often carries feelings of superiority and may act controlling or place blame. However, if the Villain is blamed, they become defensive and may switch to the role of Victim. If the Victim or Savior blames the Villain, the Victim or Savior may switch roles and become the Villain.

When I first learned about the drama triangle and its relationship to the victim mentality, I could immediately see how I had formed and contributed to many of these triangles throughout my life. Seeing when you are in the middle of one can be challenging. These dynamics form because of separation. Each person in the drama triangle operates out of their perceived need, which is often subconscious. This triangle is then held in dysfunction and by the stagnation of each participant's separation.

The roles of Victim and Villain can be more difficult to realize until the Savior comes into the dynamic. Most people have a habitual role they play in the drama triangle that reflects their childhood patterns. I have been in my fair share of Victim and Villain roles, but it is the role of the Savior that I have been particularly suited to (haha!).

If you find yourself in this role, consider it an opportunity to look more deeply at your motivations and where they come from. They are often subconscious and can take some unearthing to discover. What might alleviate the drama triangle dynamic? Awareness of the separation mentality that exists to create the triangle and the roles of each individual within it can break the spell.

Wherever you find yourself in the triangle, you can now admire and forgive the others. On the spiritual level, others in a drama triangle with you are helping you find places where you have been separated. Explore where in your life you may have been in a drama triangle or where you still might be in one. In the next section, we will learn about one more potential trap in your awareness during your growth in consciousness: spiritual bypassing.

## One Last Trap: Spiritual Bypassing

It's common for people to plateau along their spiritual journey if they seek only the higher feelings. At this stage, they may bypass the ones that don't feel good. This is another potential trap when it is done before mastering your emotions. Most spiritual principles can be utilized as a bypass. Some examples:

- *Good vibes only.*
- *Anger is a destructive emotion.*
- *You create your reality.* (You may have seen this one in this book!)

However, whether they are a spiritual bypass depends entirely on how they are used. They are spiritual bypasses when used to dismiss or judge someone else's choices, make excuses for poor behavior, or negate or suppress emotions in the self or other.

Basically, the spiritual principle being used does not match the level the person has reached. This can be part of the maturation process. Spiritual bypass can arise from a person's desire to be further ahead in their development without an authentic assessment of where they are (which can be tricky!).

The mature awareness to understand your emotional patterns and where they came from is essential. If assessment is difficult, you can usually look to the reflections in your world. Check-in with how separate you genuinely feel and how the world might be reflecting this back to you.

In the initial phases of releasing density and stuck emotions from the first three chakras, learning how to deal with emotions is exactly what it is about! At the same time, it is true that at higher levels of consciousness, your relationship to contracted feelings don't come up as often because a new level of maturation has occurred. This is because when you have fully integrated your internal polarity, you ignite a new level of creation as you begin creating with external poles.

*Check-in with yourself occasionally to seek your humble spirit. Make peace with where you are. Remember that there is no destination; the evolutions can be endless, and it is all about learning to enjoy the process. Your choices and the choices of others are their beautiful human experience. Allow yourself and others the experience of polarity for the creation of growth.*

If you have contracted emotions that come up and make you uncomfortable, acknowledge them. This is acknowledging yourself. The density is there because these parts of yourself have been stuffed down and, in the process, weigh your awareness and experience of life down.

You're noticing them gives them a path to expand and move through you to create more space. If you expand the contracting emotion to each cell of the body, creating safety and inviting it in, the amazing technology there will transmute that emotion (Playing with Polarity practice).

A practice for moving stuck emotions or a sound meditation that opens the chakras will be similar. If your Kundalini is open, this is the work that energy does to release density through the ascending chakras. If your Kundalini has not yet been opened, don't worry! Your work will make that process a lot more seamless when it does happen.

In the next section, there will be a discussion on how this chapter's themes of mind are related to the solar plexus chakra.

## Solar Plexus Chakra: I AM

The third chakra's color frequency is yellow, located in the solar plexus, right under the ribs. This is the chakra of self-experience, where themes around self-worth and self-confidence appear. This is the most important chakra for who you are right now.

This chakra represents the middle of the energetic system. It is the midpoint where we are connected both to the Earth and the universe, the above and below. It is the center of you on every level of existence.

The purpose of your separate nature is to use your uniqueness to activate your own potential to share and receive with others. You do this by being born, having many life experiences that compose a story, and returning to the self to integrate your experiences of your lifetime. We experience countless micro-loops of this pattern that all contribute to your life story.

*The highest use of your separate experience is to create in the world and then pull that experience back into yourself for integration. To be an aware creator, you need balance in your separate self.*

The solar plexus chakra is related to the pancreas, which is both a gland (it secretes hormones and digestive enzymes) and an organ (it performs functions for the body). Glucose is the body's primary energy fuel, and digestion breaks the glucose down from food and sends it to the pancreas. This organ then directs the glucose energy to all parts of the body and regulates blood sugar through insulin secretion. The pancreas strengthens the self, and the I AM and allows for balanced emotions.

If not familiar with the term, Hindus call the I AM Brahma, Buddhists call it Dharmakaya, and Christians consider it God the Father. The spirit of the God the Creator is part of every individual. Right now, this already exists within you and inhabits your solar plexus.

The pancreas and solar plexus also take in emotional energy. The emotions we receive become the foundation of the I AM of the self. This organ processes everything we feel and receive from others. This emotional information can make us feel low (in glucose or insulin) or good (having enough glucose and insulin). We exist to be in interaction with others and connect with them to feed the self.

A lack of love can create a lack of energy and emotion in the pancreas. This is not remedied by self-love but by the relationships we have. The shift needed is solely in your perspective. You can fill yourself back up by realizing and appreciating the love you do have. Focusing on the lack depletes you.

When you bring what you have into the light of your consciousness, others will match that frequency and give it to you.

*The energy generated from the solar plexus creates gravity, which is Love.*

This gravity pulls experiences and reflections from the outside to you. If not balanced, it will pull in situations that reflect your imbalances and areas that need growth back to you.

Realize that you don't have a lack of anything, and the universe will respond with abundance. This is because the universe is like its own body system; you are like one cell within that body. Nothing is separate in this perspective, only one being of energetic flow and information sharing. If the signal you are giving out is lack, it will match that signal and give you more. If you broadcast abundance, you will get more back.

## Separate Self (Ego) and I AM

It may not be easy to relate the two at first, but there is a direct connection between the separate self and the I AM presence. The *I* in the I AM is God, Unity, and Creator, and the *AM* is the individual self or separate self. The I AM presence signifies a union between the two. The *I*, then, is the universe, and the *AM* is the universe put into action by the idea of "being" projected into form.

The universe (*I*) uses vibration, the first expression of Love, to create energy that becomes matter. The purpose of the creation of matter was so separate beings could have an individual experience and then find their way back to Unity.

As mentioned before, the separate self is a tool of evolution; it is a structure through which we build our personality and have experiences. Without it, we would not have a frame of reference to relate our lives to the world. This forms the different perspectives of each human, who each holds a piece of the truth.

Without this individualized sense of self, there would be no way to acknowledge who you are in this reality. Everyone would have the same perspective and operate from oneness. That sounds great, but we are here first to experience separation, develop our personality, and then find our way back to our more spiritual nature.

Your personality was forged by your soul using specific recipe of archetypes designed to experience certain growth that it is expanding into. This means your growth path was chosen before you were born. Your personality to this point in time is an amalgam of the planetary influences/archetypes, ancestry, your human experiences, and connections with others.

Some people incarnate with a strongly unbalanced separate self, while others come in with a more integrated separate self. No path is better: each soul chooses what they need to experience for their growth and destiny in this lifetime. You can choose to balance the self to change your experience and become an aware creator of your life. This is an available choice for everyone.

Neither choice is wrong or bad. However, you still are responsible for what you create. Some people want to leave this reality for another, it's because they don't understand that they are responsible for what has manifested in their lives.

Three main types of unbalanced separate selves occur when you don't know yourself:

1. *Egoistic* separate selves occur when you try to reach outside yourself for validation. This may show up as trying to prove yourself to others (you are smarter, more evolved, or have more). Competition and comparison are typical here. This is a need to be seen by others because you can't see yourself.

2. *Egocentric* separate selves want to make themselves the center of everyone else's lives. In this situation, you need others to tell you who you are. This is common with some celebrities. People in this experience pull in the egos of others to locate themselves.

3. Minimizing yourself encourages self-doubt and keeps you sad or afraid. These are subtler ways of sabotaging yourself and creating imbalances in your solar plexus.

Acknowledge that you are the center of your own reality, and that everyone else is the center of their own story. It doesn't matter if anyone else is paying attention or what they think. Just shine in your unique way in the world!

This is easier said than done. It is a practice that you must consciously engage with every day and shift your perspective. It is practicing not being pulled off your center by others and not trying to pull others off theirs. You will notice relationships begin to change when you show up in this new way of being.

The beauty here is that your separate self is a conduit *of* and *to* the divine. Once you balance it, you create more stability in yourself, and a connection to your spirit opens. This is done first by knowing that your perspectives, understanding of reality, and beliefs are for yourself and your experience.

Further, trying to change others to be, believe, or think the way you do is an imbalanced expression from the solar plexus. You can share the Love of what you are experiencing and what is important to you without attachment to whether others take on your beliefs and perceptions. In terms of the solar plexus, this allows others to be their own experience and transmit their own uniqueness.

This is where an acquaintance with Unconditional Love begins to become important. It is defined as Loving without the need to change another. If you Love without conditions, you are Loving what is. This is the secret to balancing the solar plexus chakra and the parts of the separate self, and the I AM that exists there.

Learning how to practice Unconditional Love gives you an individual experience (through the separate self) of the divine (I AM). Unconditional Love is the frequency God uses to create, and we are learning to use this frequency to create while we are in matter (human form).

In my work, I enjoy sharing my perspectives of reality and what has worked for me. It is constantly evolving, and I hold them lightly. All my words, written or spoken, have much more content in the form of energy behind the words. These are concepts that begin to enter the realm of the wordless, the place that can be experienced but not described.

Therefore, anything presented here is an invitation for you to absorb these perspectives and transform them into your own understanding. This is the beauty of no one person having the whole truth.

There are always difficult (human perspective) and rich lessons (spiritual perspective) in the relationships we encounter. This is because others are mirroring your lessons back to you. In truth, your greatest enemy is your greatest spiritual ally. They are helping you evolve in just the right way for your highest good if you can take the opportunity presented.

When we invoke a higher perspective, appreciation is more accessible. This is most obvious in our closest relationships. Once you realize that your spiritual self chose these relationships to help you learn specific lessons during this embodiment, you can begin to hold higher solar plexus chakra interactions with them. This frees them up on some level but frees you up exponentially more.

If the goal is to continue evolving more deeply into the heart chakra, we must find balance in accepting that our unique perception of reality is valid, just as others are. Their perceptions are based on their levels of consciousness (expanded is not necessarily better, just different) and what they came to this human experience to learn.

It may seem as if more people than ever are going through a spiritual awakening, but not everyone is meant to follow a spiritual path—and certainly not your exact path. Make peace with this. Your truth is not the truth of others' and that is okay.

Applying the true nature of polarity as creation is helpful here, as it makes it easier to understand and less difficult to experience.

> *You exist in an individual reality through which your brain creates your experience. You determine how you perceive this reality, which is the foundation for moving about the world and what is possible for you.*

This can lead to a drive and, ultimately, a commitment to use your will to have expanded perceptions of your reality, leading to improved decisions for yourself and others. Many get stuck in interpersonal issues here that create a blockage. This may lead to being blocked from accessing the totality of the heart chakra. Luckily, the heart chakra has enough overlap with the solar plexus to make higher perceptions and frequencies available in difficult situations.

Individuals experience life as separate beings and relate to the external world through the solar plexus. This is a foundational step to becoming a true creator in our three-dimensional existence.

> *What each human creator makes in the world is a direct reflection of the self, and the product of each creation depends on the level of consciousness doing the creating.*

God begins as oneness and separates it into others (into poles), then the others create (through polarity), and *their* creations continue to create. This occurs on many dimensional levels. We are all part of that fractal creation pattern projected into the third dimension through the third chakra.

You are consciously engaging the work to shift the density and have deeper access to your heart's intelligence. Since this transition is directly related to the current evolution we find ourselves in, chapter 7 will begin to explore this relationship.

# Chapter Recap

## Illuminated Takeaway

*The brain and body have automatic functioning to keep us alive and safe. When combined with your awareness, presence, and knowledge that you are more than human, you begin your path to becoming a conscious creator. This leads to experiencing increased satisfaction, and opens the door to reconnecting with your deep spiritual aspects.*

The practices of admiration, gratitude, and forgiveness lay an essential foundation for the expansion we'll explore throughout the remainder of this book. Having easy access to these emotions will help you not only on the path explored here but also grant you more access to further expanded emotions.

If these are not your true practices now, you will have difficulty later. Start practicing them and watch how you free yourself!

## At this point in your journey, you may begin to experience or feel . . .

- New perspectives that create awareness of the mind itself and how perceptions affect your life
- A curiosity about how opening up to more experiences of gratitude, admiration, and forgiveness can change your life
- A spark of interest in understanding the relationship between consciousness and awareness in your life

CHAPTER 6:

# Expansion Practices for the Mental Body

Chapter 5 unveils an understanding of your power over your emotional responses that you might not be accessing. In the following expansion practices, you'll take it a step further. By creating further emotional coherence with the perspectives in chapter 5, you will activate a world of potential to experience more connection, happiness, and fulfillment.

The expansion practices in this chapter are designed to further your skills and your exploration of the solar plexus chakra. There is a new exercise from the HeartMath Institute that you can use to create heart-brain coherence during challenging situations. Your final new practices will be exercising your gratitude and admiration muscles.

The practices in the chapter will help you develop a connection with the following:

- The different parts of your mind and their strengths and using them more consciously to attain mastery

- Your body provides new physical awareness as you spend more and more time in your center, as the center of your expereince
- More felt emotions, such as admiration, to gain greater access to emotions overall

As with the previous practices, it is suggested to take 4 weeks to become proficient in the new exercises before moving on.

## Practice Overview and Checklist

### Daily Meditation

- Add the solar plexus chakra meditation exercise below to your routine.
- Rotate the additional practices of gratitude and admiration in your meditations.
- You are also welcome to revisit previous additional practices as daily meditation options to make sure you are mastering them all.

### Daily Journal

- Check in with your experience. Note any recent mental or emotional contractions, expansions, or questions that you may be reflecting on.
- Reflect on any notable experiences you have during new exercises.
- Moment of expansion: What is your experience when you are out of your center? How does it feel when you operate from your center? Is any other awareness about your experience or the world bubbling to the surface? Contemplate what these new practices offer your awareness and daily life.

## Tools to Practice Throughout Your Daily Life

- Watching the Thinker
- Steps to Change a Pattern
- Movement
- Playing with Polarity
- Forgiveness
- Connect with the Felt Sense of Hormones
- HeartMath's Freeze-Frame Technique*
- Gratitude*
- Admiration*

*New practice

## Add to Your Weekly Meditation: Solar Plexus Chakra Humming

The solar plexus includes themes of self-mastery. When this chakra is clear and balanced, so will be your "doing" in the world. You will have access to confidence and the energy to engage with the world.

Perform your normal daily meditation by readying your space, creating safety and comfort, breathwork, humming, and completing your practice through the solar plexus chakra. You can play with doing this meditation with or without humming. See what you prefer.

Now add the solar plexus chakra portion as you continue to hum:

1. Imagine the flow of powerful orange creation energy moving like lava up to feed the solar plexus. This is bringing the light of the creator into your belly. The plexus is the core of your being, where the energy transforms into a yellow shining sun. This is your center: you are this powerful, warm

glow out into the world, a magnet for what you create in your world. It is also the center of everything. Feel the Love that already exists in your life. You don't need the story of where the Love is coming from—just connect with the Love.

2. Remember, this is where the *I* of your higher aspects and the *AM* of your human self exist together to form the I AM. The I AM is your ego. Bring your awareness to the I AM presence here. Feel the completed consciousness residing in your solar plexus radiate like solar light in all directions. Take a deep breath and shine even brighter now. Feel the eternal strength here, pulsing with energy and excitement to be, interact, and do in the world. Take a deep breath and shine even more!

3. As you feel the process come to completion, finish your practice as before. Keep your eyes closed and do a physical body scan with your hands, massaging and touching your body parts to ground yourself back in the body and create comfort within. If you feel pulled, sit with your experience and see if anything arises.

Journal about new experiences, sensations, or insights you had during or after meditation. You are encouraged to connect with your inner sun daily to reorient yourself to center. You have all you need inside already. Anchor yourself there and enjoy the experience of life.

Next are your shiny new additional practices to add to your daily meditations. They will continue to develop a sense of flow in life. Throughout month 3, you will rotate the practices of gratitude and admiration to your daily meditations. You will start all meditations as you always have with the following: readying yourself, creating safety and comfort, breathwork, humming, and watching the thinker. Then, add one of the following new practices. Close the meditation as usual and journal about what arises.

# Gratitude

After your meditation, it is suggested that you start a gratitude practice as part of your journaling. This can be part of a daily meditation and a felt activity throughout the day. Realize the moment you are grateful for someone or something you have experienced. Days ebb and flow, and sometimes, it can be challenging to access the feeling of gratitude, or you may find this to be true as you start the practice. Know that wherever you start is the perfect place to begin.

The words *gratitude* and *appreciation* are often used synonymously, and we all have a definition based on our experiences. For more clarity, let's bring in the specific definition of appreciation.

*Appreciation* is the "recognition of the quality, value, significance, or magnitude of people and things; a sensitive awareness; increase in value."

*Gratitude* is "a felt sense of wonder, thankfulness, and appreciation for life. It can be expressed to others as well as impersonal (nature) or nonhuman sources (God, animals, cosmos.)"

(Both definitions come from *Emmons's Gratitude and the Science of Positive Psychology.*)

You will continue to develop these emotions in further chapters, as gratitude is related to love and helps us open up to our experiences, be present, and enjoy life more fully.

To get you started, here are twenty questions to help cultivate gratitude.

1. What are you most grateful for at this moment?
2. What are you grateful for in this current phase of life?
3. What about yourself are you grateful for?

4. What relationships in your life bring you feelings of stability that make you feel grateful?

5. What or who made you laugh or smile today?

6. Who really listens when you talk, and how does that affect you?

7. What is a problematic situation that yielded much growth for you, and how does that make you feel?

8. What basic needs do you not have to worry about meeting today?

9. Have you had a chance to help someone recently, and how did that make you feel?

10. Is there something you really enjoy that you get to experience daily that you take for granted?

11. How does nature make you feel grateful?

12. What about today? Has it been better than yesterday, last week, or last month?

13. What aspect of your physical health do you feel grateful for?

14. What happened today, yesterday, this week, month, or year that you're grateful for?

15. What are your favorite things about your city, town, or state?

16. What are your talents that you are most grateful for, and what do you enjoy about applying them?

17. What close relationships are you grateful for in your life?

18. What aspect of your childhood do you feel most grateful for?

19. What's one thing you've enjoyed about your job recently?

20. What experience or opportunity have you had that makes you feel grateful?

You have already created the felt experience of more gratitude in your life! Next, try the following exercise in meditation or daily life to help you apply the higher-frequency feelings of admiration to your world.

# Admiration

Let's first connect with the definition of *admiration*.

*Admiration* is "a feeling of strong approval or delight with regard to someone or something," or "the state of being viewed with such approval or delight."

(from The American Heritage Dictionary of the English Language, 5th Edition)

Here are some potential scenarios to interact with admiration:

1. Begin to use admiration and gratitude practices every day with the goal of using them in every interaction. Find something delightful about someone else. You can start small by injecting a few compliments into your conversations. Notice how that connects you with the other person and creates harmony and warmth for you both.

2. When in a disagreement with another, remember admiration and your center.

   There is an old story about when a wiseman was once asked "Why do people yell at each other?" The wiseman responded, "Because their hearts are so far apart that they can no longer hear each other."

   The wiseman goes on to say, "That when your hearts are very close, you only need a whisper to be heard."

   This exemplifies what is occurs in all disagreements. Frist find your center and feel that you are the center of your experience. Then bring your hearts closer with the practice of admiration. Be the one that starts to hear the other. Then thank the other for hearing you and return the admiration back and forth until you can speak about the disagreement with your hearts closer. The chances of finding resolution from this place increases exponentially.

3. Cement it in by remembering the center of your experience in your solar plexus. After your practice, feel delighted for the breakthroughs you have accomplished, balanced connection with others, and the freedom you are opening for yourself.

Now, you are beginning a deeper metamorphosis process! Have these be your go-to practices daily to shift old patterns.

Journal about your admiration practice. Was it difficult or easy? Did it bring in any new awareness?

## HeartMath's Freeze-Frame Technique (FFT)

You will hear more about the HeartMath Institute and the fantastic research they are doing in chapter 7. This institute developed a simple tool to use whenever you want to regain emotional balance during a difficult situation more quickly and consciously. It lets you nip things in the bud before contracting emotions cause exhausting drama. It offers the ability to develop creative solutions from a higher perspective and with improved discernment.

The idea is to engage the part of your brain that can see what you are experiencing as a movie and "freeze" it in your mind's eye. Then, from that third-person vantage point, you shift your attention to your heart center and feel a sense of appreciation that you generate. This helps bring in a detachment from the experience and allows for emotional re-regulation.

You are, in essence, hijacking your negative emotional response and moving it toward coherence. Try it out!

1. Disengage from stressful emotions and thoughts that arise by observing and "freezing" the moment in your mind.

2. Focus your awareness on your heart center in the middle of your chest. Visualize the movement of your breath as you breathe into that space. On the exhale, feel your breath leave through the solar plexus. Repeat three to five times.

3. Authentically self-activate a positive feeling, such as appreciation or gratitude. You can do this by thinking of something you are genuinely grateful for. Maybe you identified something that conjures these feelings during the gratitude exercise in this chapter. Remember that you are responsible for your reactions and feelings.

4. Feel yourself return to your center in your solar plexus. Remember that you are the sun, the center, of your experience.

5. Ask yourself for a perspective or action that would rebalance your system.

6. Sense any changes in emotions or subtle higher observations. Try to maintain this space of increased coherence.

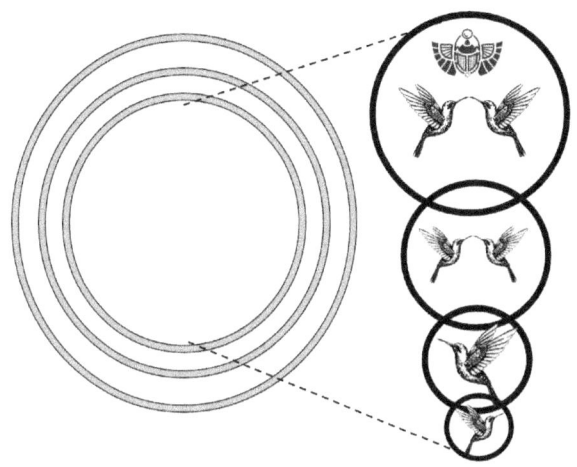

# Fourth Octave:
# Chapters 7 and 8

### Into the Heart (Astral Plane)

You do not need to hold on to or seek love—there is an infinite source. You are remembering that your consciousness is Love and that you can use that Love to create. The energy of Love constantly moves through creation.

**Old Perspective:** *An unconscious belief, as in "I need other people and things to feel loved."*

**New Perspective:** *A conscious engagement, as in "I am the technology that both creates and experiences Love."*

This marks the threshold to working with your existence on the Astral Plane. It represents the transition from the third-dimension to fourth-dimensional consciousness.

# CHAPTER 7

# Consciousness Moves from the Mind to the Heart

*The world is full of magic things, patiently waiting for
your senses to grow sharper.*

—W. B. Yeats

Love is an omnipresent force in the universe, waiting for you
to engage your technology.

The focus of the previous chapters has been to clear density from
your mind, nervous system, and first three chakras. This has
occurred mainly on the physical plane. You have been learning to
observe patterns, take responsibility for what you are creating, integrate lessons, and apply them in your life. It has been an important
foundation for utilizing the full technology of the heart that we will
explore in the remaining chapters of this book.

Feel a sense of accomplishment for meeting the heart in a new and
deeper way! Know that you are poised for more.

Now you see that the emotional or mental patterns you have observed were not who you are. They are adaptations (not evolutions) that served a purpose at one time but have now become obsolete. You feel an increased sense of freedom and flexibility in your emotional and mental experiences. You may feel a satisfaction in taking responsibility for your life and are spending more time being the center of your experience.

At the same time, you have been developing your hormonal system to have more access to higher-frequency feelings and their associated hormones. The goal is not to be in bliss 100% of the time. It is to realize that all emotions are a type of Love at different frequencies and are a response to your experience. You have tools and perspectives to give context to them. Now the objective is to bring balance to them with the assistance of the heart chapters.

However, this phase in your development could also bring internal and external separations. For example, you may experience an internal struggle over wanting to live more and more by spiritual principles, yet still having stagnating patterns without an awareness of them yet. Or there could be interpersonal separations between family members and friends or even an inspired shift in your career. The appearance of anger and frustration is often a signal that you have begun the work but have not yet initiated some of the difficult separations you need.

This means your frequency is shifting, and it is common to be afraid of change. As long as you remain attached to certain people, places, or things, you will fear losing them. Even as you work through this book, you may fear expanding and leaving people behind or experiencing agitation. Know that this is a sign that you are ready to evolve. Set your intention to surrender and courageously move towards the beautiful changes that await you.

You are aligning more with the frequency of your True Essence. This is what you are beyond societal programming, unconscious patterns, and other artificial separations. When you let go of these structures, your inner light can begin to shine through. This is the frequency of your beingness. This is both your True Essence and the Love it creates that radiates through you.

This beingness is always inside, you can see how it can be difficult to access due to acquired densities in your subtle bodies. This is why much focus has been on clearing and clarifying the way for this essence to shine through. At this point in your journey, the gateway to further accessing your human technology exists in the utilization of the incredible machinery of the heart and its chakra.

Let's consider the word hormone's etymology, or the source. Its roots are in the Greek noun *hormon*, which means "that which sets in motion" or, in verb form, "to impel, urge on." Its other root is *horme*, or "onset or impulse."

> *Using these definitions leads to a greater understanding that hormones and the love you feel are your impetus and energy, not just for procreation but for all you create in your life. Without this impulse, there is little drive to "be" and no motivation to "do" in the world.*

This is the crux of many issues in our modern society: "doing" to merely survive creates suffering. We can thrive if we can "be" and "do" with access to our True Essence. You can even extend the discussion to emotions in general, as they are energy creators in our systems and out to the world through our chakras. When the path for this energy is clear to flow, we are optimized. This is the state where you can radiate the Love of your being into the world and everything you do.

This is precisely what the heart is for. It is the balance point between what you think (mind), do (body), feel (soul), and what you receive and give, as you will learn in this chapter. By harmonizing these parts of self and continuing to take responsibility for your experience, more consciousness opens.

## Using Our Current Hardware for Conscious Evolution

You are helping your senses to grow sharper! By applying Yeats' quote at the beginning of the chapter, again you find that you are accessing that for which you already have the hardware. You are being awakened. These technologies just needed perspectives, understandings, and practices to begin to engage. Integrating our earlier discussions of evolution and your innate technology now brings our journey into the present.

> *It is essential to remember that the unbalanced separate self is not the villain in your story—it's just a tool to identify unresolved issues and find your center. As long as this mechanism runs your life unbalanced, your progress will stagnate.*

The magic enters when you begin to stay in the center of yourself, not seeking anything from the outside. Have you begun to feel this difference? With a centered sense of self, you will continue using the established machinery to advance evolution with your conscious participation.

The next step is to turn inward to the actual source of all our experiences. As we continue to foster higher emotions, we can then realize that the movement from mind to heart is the door for our expansion and signifies a deeper relationship with our whole selves.

> *From the spiritual perspective, as we saw in the concept of polarity, all your experiences are a projection from your internal states*

*and soul lessons, played out on a stage of sorts in front of you. Through the conscious development of your heart, you can learn how to navigate your internal and external realities and experiences effortlessly.*

The secret is in our growing awareness that we control our internal and external experiences. It is like when Glinda tells Dorothy in *The Wizard of Oz* that the ability to go home was always within her. The ability to come home to yourself and to step into deep creatorship is here, right now! It just takes a little work (play).

As more experiences of expanded feelings allow access to the full spectrum of Love, you cultivate an opening to the ability to live from the heart. Once you have matured the self to this level, you can take this further and merge all the separate selves (from this life, ancestors, and past lives). This integrates your personality with the larger truth of who you are. As this occurs you open to your deeper capabilities. This is the process of realization, and its progression is based on the trust built within yourself and with the universe. Really, it is all waiting for you to access it.

The exciting news is that research is beginning to show the importance of the heart's technology and energy field. Some of this wonderful research in this area came from the HeartMath Institute (HMI), which has been studying heart-brain coherence for more than twenty years.

## Science Begins to Understand the Technology of the Heart

Positive emotions are often correlated with spiritual experiences. Love, appreciation, and compassion can all be felt in connection with the divine, and this is no accident! These feelings help remind us of our True Selves and connection to everything during our time as humans.

This is not reserved for the "special people" most organized religions may profess. Everyone can remember the totality of what they are, but for most people, these experiences are sporadic and inconsistent because those people cannot emotionally regulate.

Lack of emotional regulation can manifest as emotions you think you cannot control, but another extreme is near complete repression of emotional function. HMI describes emotional regulation as a heart rhythm coherence that increases the synchronization of the heart with the brain. This leads to greater cognitive functioning, emotional regulation, positive health impacts, and increased spiritual connectedness.

In a place of coherence, you have a deep sense of peace, a feeling of balance within yourself, and a greater connection to your surroundings. This creates clarity where you were previously confused and a sense of general well-being while inner conflict is minimized. The beauty of heart-brain coherence unveiled! How exciting it is that it can be studied.

> In an early article, HMI founder Doc Lew Childre wrote that "Positive emotional states may indeed be key to optimal functioning, enhancing nearly all spheres of human experience. . . . [They can] improve health, increase longevity, increase cognitive flexibility and creativity, facilitate 'broad-minded coping' and innovative problem solving, and promote helpfulness, generosity, and effective cooperation."

Childre also postulates that these positive emotional states may be the key to further advancements for our species. If you remember our discussion about the brain in chapter 5, the unevolved neurons of the corpus callosum may be waiting for activation via a more heart-based way of living.

Yet, at this moment in our society, most people's days are devoid of these feelings. The stresses of everyday life keeps most anxious and detached from more expanded feelings. The remedy is to purposefully recondition the emotional system to experience more expanded emotions until it becomes the norm. Many of the practices at the end of the chapters have been moving you in this direction to develop your access.

HMI has taken it further and created biofeedback devices to help you understand what heart-brain coherence feels like. This can be useful when starting, and I recommend these devices to many, especially those new to breathwork or meditation.

What is it exactly that keeps you from coherence? It is nothing more than the free rein of our emotions and an unbalanced separate self that distracts us with the noise they create. Most people spend their lives with busy minds, meaning our neural pathways are primed for more of the same experiences.

Luckily, it is within your power to change this. People on a spiritual path become aware of this, so they dedicate a significant amount of time to meditating, implementing breathwork, and chanting. These practices create more emotional and physical coherence and open them to higher emotions. Indeed, having a conscious practice creates more coherence; it shifts our perspectives to understand that this can be our baseline.

The first step is to recognize your response when you experience a contracted emotion. This emotion is a signal to act so you can regulate to a heightened state. It is a beautiful system when it is understood for what it is! However, emotional alarms may stay on when you have an unregulated baseline state or coherence, creating hypersensitivity that intensifies emotional ups and downs.

Again, most people exist in this state for much of their lives. Moreover, many don't realize what is happening. If you aim to access these expanded emotional states indefinitely, you must have practices that train your nervous system to maintain control in triggering situations. This gives you greater adaptability and flexibility to greet whatever experiences you attract to you.

## The Brilliance of the Heart

The importance of hormones in our evolution has been considered, as hormones contribute to the transformation from living in your mind to occupying the beingness available in the body and the heart. But did you know the human heart does much more than pump blood through our veins? It has neurons (brain cells!)—more than forty thousand of them—which means it is part of the nervous system and can drive the creation and secretion of hormones.

The heart is also a sensing organ and can independently learn, remember, and make decisions based on stimuli. These inputs are sent to the brain and affect the function of the autonomic nervous system and are at the core of our emotional experience.

As a human and mammal, you experience reality more through the heart than through your separate self (solar plexus) in your body. This is because our hormonal systems evolved to be a fundamental part of our interaction and understanding of the world, as previously described. Mammals navigate the world through the five senses, emotions, and hormone responses. These then create memories that get stored in the heart.

*It is most straightforward to relate to the heart because feelings are the language of the mammalian brain that makes sense of your experience and reality.*

Everything you have experienced as a human since you were an initial cell in our mother's womb creates a memory of a sensation that is stored. An interesting report that may corroborate the heart as an organ of memory appears in the book *The Heart's Code* by Dr. Paul Pearsall. Pearsall had a heart transplant recipient who experienced many significant and specific personality changes.

Before the surgery, the man openly professed racist beliefs and was not interested in classical music. Then after the surgery, he was drawn to befriend African Americans at work. People that he had previously avoided. He also secretly began listening to classical violin concertos.

Later, upon learning more about who the donor was, the patient found that these changes he was experiencing lined up with the donor's personality. The heart donor was a male African American classical violinist! There are many similar stories like this one. They illustrate that you are storing memories from your heart's experience, creating your personality and how you interact with the world.

The physical beating of the heart activates glands to secrete hormones and then to the organs and chakras to create energy. When the glands create hormones, they travel through the bloodstream on the pulse of the heartbeat to reach the entire body.

Your heart beats faster when you experience an opening, connection with someone, or loving situation. This disperses hormones throughout the whole body that correlate with the experience. It can feel like an expansion of the heart; in this way, we associate our experience with the beating of our heart. You are your own biofeedback device!

> *Your specific response is based on past conditioning, and you follow the established pattern unless you choose to repurpose the pattern with awareness and perspective.*

The beating of your heart helps you perceive, through feeling, the contrast (poles) of reality and relate it to your experience. Each heartbeat carries two sounds: the first expands emotion out into the world (positive pole) and the second that contracts (negative pole) information back into the self. In this way, our emotional experiences are projected out into the world by the heart, which senses reality and sends information back.

> *This is a fractal of what the Creator is also doing. A pulse constantly expands and contracts from the heart (center) of creation in God, you, and every living being.*

Remember that evolution can be as simple as a perspective shift. Everyone reading this book has had this experience and every moment is an opportunity if you are aware.

Let yourself see all these expanding technologies at your disposal, with Love being the energy between it all. Now you can begin to understand that Love manifests form. As many people do, you can manifest your life from an unbalanced, separate self. This is a perfectly acceptable experience of life because you chose your experience. However, the current energy of evolution is moving quickly beyond these patterns to something new.

Continued alignment with yourself encourages encounters with all the facets of Love; your experience's creation, when coherent, can create your reality beyond your wildest dreams. Developing your sense of self will put you in this creator's seat of your reality. Manifesting from this place will not only be more effective but will be more in alignment with all.

This is what I mean by *Love manifests form.* Whether you are aligned or not, Love is manifesting form in different levels of frequency. The opportunity is in having full access to the technology of the heart and your being (or True Essence), you align with the full potential of the human form and the universe. Let's continue to explore this technology from the perspective of the heart's energy center.

## The Heart Chakra: I AM into I AM Love

The heart chakra is associated with the color frequency green and is in the center of the chest. This chakra is part of a circuit in our chest fed by the gravity of Love created in our solar plexus. This gravity is pulsed out to the world by heartbeats moving through the circuit.

*A balanced, separate self is needed to find harmony in the heart.*

Your left hand receives energy from the world around you, and the right hand creates a flow of energy out to the world. Everything you receive goes through the physical heart and the chakra in the center of your chest.

The universe is in a constant energetic flow, and when you receive something, energy needs to be given to return to balance. Your heart circuit creates this balance. When you give, the universe gives you energy back at the same frequency as you gave. Much like an echo. Whatever is being given could be a masterpiece, although if you made it with sadness, you are giving that sadness with a beautiful exterior. Then you receive more sadness in return.

In another example, if you are giving all your time to others and feel as if you are not receiving "enough" back, then the frequency of the emotion from which you are giving may be blocking the experience you want. This is especially true with complaining. If you give and constantly complain about it, then the universe will keep sending you more to complain about. It creates a stuck pattern.

The universe moves energy and works to fill the voids of frequency for balance. Just like in your body's cells, automatic functions send energy and nutrients where they are most needed to maintain homeostasis. For example, if you want to receive joy, you must first give joy.

Of course, we each have more than one emotion at one time. There is a relationship between the different emotions and different chakras, and the heart circuit manifests what you receive and how you give. However, when you identify the emotions under the energy you give, you can choose different frequency emotions from which to create your world.

One way to begin to shift an emotion is through laughter. Laugh at yourself! Look at how silly it is how we suffer in this human experience. This may be a difficult practice at first. However, it allows the emotions to become buoyant and begins to create movement and expansion of your frequency. This begins a new way, one where you take responsibility for yourself and your creations.

Received emotions (energy) from your environment needs to move and flow. If we are unaware, we sometimes want to hold on to an emotion out of fear of losing it. When you try to keep it, it deposits in your liver to be processed as if it is part of your personality. However, it cannot be processed because it is not part of the self. It came from outside of the self.

When the liver keeps and processes an external emotion, it can turn into anger, rage, or hate. When you keep an emotion, you created in resonance with yourself, it nourishes the body's organs. When you keep emotions that were given to you but that you were meant to continue to move, you create a link of attachment with the person, object, or animal. These links of attachment form in the solar plexus in this way and confuse your sense of self.

## Heart Circuit

4) **Release: Right Hand**
**Information/Energy/Emotions**

1) **Receive: Left Hand**
**Information/Energy/Emotions**

**2) Process & 3) Absorb**

The heart circuit of an individual is designed for the flow of energy as depicted above and rides on the pulse of the physical heartbeat. Here are the main steps:

- The left hand receives energy in the form of vibration through secondary hand chakras;
- Then it moves to the physical heart to be understood and stored;
- It pulses it quickly as frequency through the heart chakra, connecting with the solar plexus and modulating the gravity there;
- On that same pulse, the right hand directs energy out into the world;
- The gravity of the heart and the frequency put into the world then determines what vibration reflects back to the left hand, and the cycle starts again.

All occurring as quickly as one full heartbeat!

This energy then moves through the network of many individuals in the web of the collective consciousness on our planet. We receive energy from food, emotions, and thoughts. Our role is to let the information in, transform it, and give it away.

The heart circuit is like a digestive system for all the different energies. When you consume food, it is broken down into parts to be absorbed by different organs, and then what your body does not need is discharged into the toilet. Although the waste you create is useful for other life, as compost. The energy keeps moving in this way.

This also happens on the level of the mind. When a person shares an idea, you let it into your mind, understand it to some degree by breaking it into parts, and then transform it within your perspective (much like digestion). It becomes a part of you because you transformed the needed parts to resonate with you. Then, you share your version of the idea out in your life and disregard what did not resonate.

Then, there is also a flow and transformation on an emotional level. It is easiest to see with our experience of love. When a partner gives you love and you let that emotion in, it activates a cascade of hormones (as discussed in chapter 3) that transmutes the frequency of love that came in to be in resonance with you. Then, you give your transformed love back to your partner. Your individual circuits create a larger circuit.

There is no bad or good energy for the circuit, only polarity, balance, and your awareness to create your experience. Fast-frequency inputs takes a lot of energy for the body to process, and it is okay to have slow-frequency energy to experience. Fast-frequency energy could be love (emotions), an exciting new idea (mind), or a strawberry from your garden (food).

You are looking for the balance. When imbalance occurs, the flow shuts down. This can look like constipation, which is holding on to food, love, or ideas due to a fear that others would reject or misunderstand them. In each one of these, fear stops the movement of energy.

Stuck energy can lead to addictions that appear as attachments in the solar plexus. On the physical level, you can get attached to foods or other substances. On the emotional level, you can become attached to an emotion, which keeps you subconsciously trying to recreate a situation. On the mind level, you can become attached to a belief even if you know it is not serving you.

An attachment is unhealthy only when it is dysfunctional. You can be attached to your parents, pets, children, friends, and partners in a healthy way. However, when you can't stay away from a situation that is hurting you in some way (physically, mentally, or emotionally), then it is an unhealthy attachment.

There is a significant relationship between the solar plexus and heart chakra. If you don't have a balanced sense of self with *you* at the center of your experience, the heart chakra circuit will not be balanced, and you will draw imbalance into your life. When you are unclear about who you are, you send this message to the heart and exchange confused energy with the world.

When there is balance in your solar plexus, the energy that feeds the heart chakra is purified and clear. You can use the heart circuit to create more from your True Self. This is a deepening in being the creator of your reality.

The central theme of our planetary evolution is a more profound activation and access in the heart chakra. For this to occur, it has been necessary to clear the channel from the first three chakras. Then, you can effectively use the energies generated from your human self and the Universal Love that flows from your higher aspects, allowing you to become the creator of your own experience. It begins as self-regulation that will bring increased coherence and health.

In the next chapter's expanding practices, you will bring all this together and apply it to yourself in a creative project called Tuning Your Energetic Heart.

In the next section, we will return to our focus on different types of Love and allow you to connect with a felt sense of each. Think about our discussion about the heart circuit: energy comes in, you process it, absorb it, and finally release it in a new form useful to another and the world.

## Meet Love in Multiple Contexts

As mentioned earlier, most people think of Love in terms of romantic Love first; then they consider the attachment bond between parent and child. These are some of the strongest bonds you can have on the human level, but I would also like to familiarize you with other types of Love. This is by no means an exhaustive list, as there are 267 words for Love in Sanskrit alone, but there are nine different types according to both modern and ancient Greeks.

Also included are questions to facilitate a deeper connection with the different frequencies associated with each word. As you consider each type of Love, feel what it's like to experience its expression. You are welcome to journal about your experience if you would like. Notice the differences in how each one makes you feel.

This helps open and utilize a new dimension of learning and knowing that most do not access day-to-day. Precisely what you are activating with this book. Doing this will help you gauge where you are on that scale. If you have not personally felt a particular type of Love, you can bring in other stories or archetypes that help you feel and experience it.

Let's access these feelings to better understand the broader and higher frequency scale of what Love is.

## *Pragma*: Enduring Love

*Pragma* is a love that takes time to grow and establish. This love is responsible and dedicated. *Pragma* usually includes a commitment after a bond formed during shared experiences.

Feel the stability and trust encoded in this type of love. You can lean into this love and create more profound levels of safety with others. What has been your most significant example of feeling *pragma*?

## *Ludus*: Playful Love

*Ludus* has a youthful quality to it. The excitement of being around someone is mainly correlated with the early flirting stage or childhood friendships.

Words like *sweet, innocent*, and *lively* can typically be used to describe the feelings of this type of love. Did you have a childhood friend that you had *ludus* with? Or perhaps there was a light-hearted flirtation that you experienced. Remember what that felt like.

## *Philia*: Deep Friendship

*Philia* is a platonic, long-lasting friendship that deepens into love. It is associated with deep trust, comradery, and appreciation for the other. The Greeks valued this more than *eros* (romantic love).

Have you experienced a friendship where you would do anything for the other person? A feeling of deep comradery and resonance with others accompanies this interaction. What has your experience of this been?

## *Storge*: Family Love

*Storge* encompasses both love between immediate family and close friends. It differs from *philia* in that it is encouraged by blood relations, childhood bonding, and familiarity.

This could be the family you were born into, your chosen family, or others who feel like family. Either way, a bond is formed from knowing this person over a long period and understanding them through different life phases. What does *storge* love feel like to you?

## *Mania*: Obsessive Love

*Mania* is an out-of-balance dependency on another. You may have experienced this during your first love. When you were young, did you have a crush that felt like an obsession?

## *Philautia*: Self-Love

Our relationship with ourselves is important in our human experience as we saw in the "Solar Plexus Chakra" discussion. Being in your center is self-love. Further cultivation of *philautia* will yield positive self-esteem and confidence while improving our interactions with others. Having increased levels of self-love allows the love of others to permeate you deeper.

What is your current relationship to self-love? Has this relationship been recently evolving and in what ways? When have you felt the most self-love? How do you show yourself self-love?

## *Eros*: Passionate Love

This is the passion and attraction that creates exhilarating feelings. Eros is often the type of love that occurs during the initial stages of romance. Think of a time when you were falling in love. What was it like to experience the exhilaration?

## *Agape*: Universal Love

*Agape* has been described as a compassionate Love for all people. It is the Universal Love that is given without wanting anything in return. Buddha, Jesus, and other masters have exemplified this. It is synonymous with Unconditional Love.

Have you ever felt *agape*? Nature is an excellent place to access this specific type of Love. When you are in nature, and your heart space feels opened to more than you usually experience, this is a taste of *agape*. Some report that the Love between self and a pet feels like this type of Unconditional Love. In the next chapter, the Practice of Unconditional Love will help guide you further.

## Loving Reflection

How easy or difficult was that for you?

What are you letting yourself experience, and how are you holding yourself back because of contracting past experiences? Use one of your previously learned tools or practices from previous chapters to move through contractions.

Does the mere thought of some of these types of love make you feel a contraction in your heart?

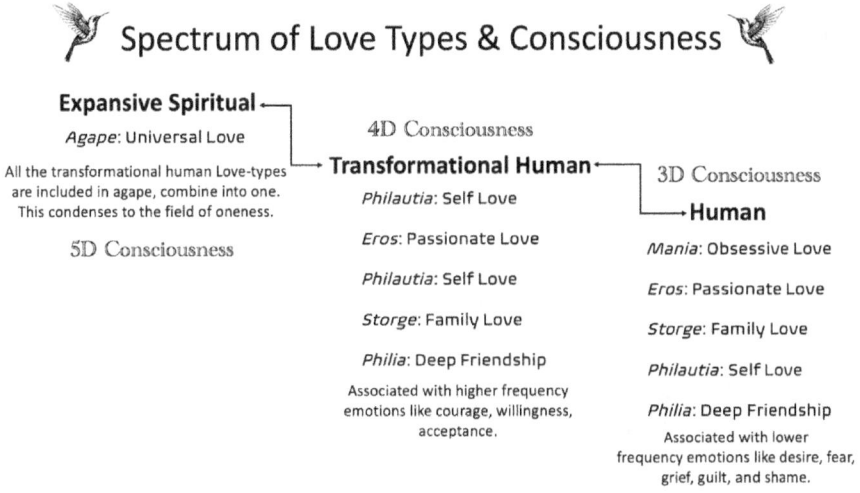

### Spectrum of Love Types & Consciousness

**Expansive Spiritual**

*Agape*: Universal Love

All the transformational human Love-types are included in agape, combine into one. This condenses to the field of oneness.

5D Consciousness

4D Consciousness

**Transformational Human**

*Philautia*: Self Love

*Eros*: Passionate Love

*Philautia*: Self Love

*Storge*: Family Love

*Philia*: Deep Friendship

Associated with higher frequency emotions like courage, willingness, acceptance.

3D Consciousness

**Human**

*Mania*: Obsessive Love

*Eros*: Passionate Love

*Storge*: Family Love

*Philautia*: Self Love

*Philia*: Deep Friendship

Associated with lower frequency emotions like desire, fear, grief, guilt, and shame.

*Love is the energy that creates all emotions. All the different emotions are just Love in different frequencies. It is the expression that has created everything in the universe.*

The above image details the different Love types with levels of consciousness: third, fourth, or higher dimensional consciousness. This means your consciousness can be solely in the typical, three-dimensional reality.

Each dimension is just a different perspective. You can have a perfect human experience while remaining in third-dimensional consciousness for your whole life. There is no judgment for the poles or frequencies you choose to experience in your life's creation. Introducing the expanded versions of emotions shows you the choices available to expand your toolbox and create more freedom.

Third-dimensional consciousness is the mode most experience on the planet—autopilot combined with feelings of separation. This is associated with love that contains denser-frequency emotions like desire, fear, grief, guilt, and shame. These experiences of love often involve the need for an object or person to complete oneself. They are still experiences of Love!

This corresponds to lower vibrational experiences related to the bigger energy of Love. Take hate, for example. At first, it seems to be the opposite of Love. However, it is actually lower vibrational Love that occurs due to an absence of love when there is a want for it.

Trauma bonding is a term that refers to a relationship where there is a deep bond coupled with some sort of abuse, whether physical or emotional. In this entangled bond, the abused continues to stay often because their loss of self-esteem leads to unhealthy mental patterns. This is very much the drama triangle at work, forming an unhealthy attachment in the solar plexus.

If you find yourself in third-dimensional consciousness and want to create a higher-vibration experience, the way out is through higher-frequency emotions like courage, willingness, and acceptance. These will lead you to find appreciation, purpose, passion, and meaning to catapult you into fourth-dimensional consciousness and make different choices for your reality. The more you practice this, the more brain structures will develop that allow access to them and hold these states for longer.

When applied to more situations in your life, a readiness develops to meet these types of Love at a higher frequency. More fulfillment opens when relating to the world through Love. After this occurs, access to Universal Love begins to open. This is a frequency that is ever present and permeates all things. When you meet this wholeness of Love, you will find that you feel not one emotion but *all emotions* in one place at one time.

> *When this happens, however, you will not be overwhelmed with all the experiences. This is a zero-point energy state, a field, and a feeling of neutrality. This is also what is termed the void, where creation starts. A tiny point in your heart space corresponds to and connects with this place.*

If you have any judgment, you cannot connect with Universal Love. Judgment occurs when you are operating from one perspective. You need to have a broader perspective to access Universal Love. However, it isn't easy to access if you vibrate solely in third-dimensional consciousness. Learn how to use the polarity (high frequency and low frequency) emotions to create the experience you want.

Notice that the arrows in the Spectrum of Love diagram are bidirectional. Before you were human, you were in and a part of Universal Love. Your soul came deeper and deeper into density to have its third-dimensional experience and to taste what that consciousness is like. Now, the mastery during our evolution is being embodied while you access more fourth-dimensional consciousness and above! Consciousness can go either way—expand into Love or contract into love. It is all still Love and experience.

Here, we have reached the extent to which our scientific minds understand love because science generally relies on the five primary senses to synthesize the perception of our reality. In chapters 9 and 10, you will receive deeper understanding regarding your intuitive senses. These are the mundane five senses expanded to receive more information.

You will also gain tools to work beyond your mind to seek, resonate, and even begin to "see" what is beyond form. You likely already have experiences that may be considered intuitive. This can look like an inner knowing, seeing, or feeling.

# Chapter Recap

## Illuminated Takeaway

*The opportunity to lift the energy from your ever balancing separate self to make room for your True Essence is here in your heart!*

This chapter introduced multiple concepts to approach a greater understanding of what the technology of the heart is. First, your feelings create energy for all that you do through the heart. The heart is like a second brain, complete with neurons, and is part of your hormonal system. You are recording all of your experiences since the beginning of your life through the emotions felt here.

Furthermore, the heart is a circuit. Frequencies enter through one hand, then get transformed by your heart and recorded, and the energy moves out in all that you do. Unconditional Love includes every emotion at different frequencies. You are constantly experiencing a part of Love, no matter the emotion.

Levels of dimensional consciousness correspond to different frequencies of Love. You can choose your experience by changing the frequency of the emotion you feel.

Although much of your experience is based on conditioning from the past, the opportunity here is that once you understand the heart's capabilities as an emotional recording and transforming device, you can consciously utilize this innate technology to shape your reality and life experiences. By directing the frequencies and emotions you feel and emanate from your heart, you have the power to manifest more clearly. This self-mastership unlocks your True Essence - the pure beingness that resides beneath conditioned patterns.

In the next chapter's expansion practices, you will connect with the technology of your heart like never before. You will tune in to, clarify, connect, and create through your heart with new awareness and purpose.

**At this point in your journey, you may begin to experience . . .**

- New understandings of how the level of consciousness of your mind has affected your life
- Perspectives that open up the intelligence of the heart and are part of our evolution
- A curiosity about how this is currently manifesting in your life and what is possible
- A spark of interest in how your life will change as you connect more deeply with the expanded aspects of your heart

Everyone is born with energetic sensitivities, though they remain mostly underdeveloped. Many who realize they have these additional senses must learn to develop them and find they are superpowers.

For example, an empath has a heightened sense of feeling. They are sensitive to the energy of others and the world around them. At times, this may be so overwhelming they limit their own life experience. For them, it may feel like "too much." Now, imagine you are an empath at a costume party. The costume adds a layer of energetic protection, as you may feel less pressure to mingle with others.

However, your energy is still mingling! You can feel the energy of the entire event before you enter the building: all the excitement and the conversations the people in attendance. You also may feel individuals' emotions, from excitement to insecurity. At the same time, there is also music, drinks, and food that add to the activity.

That is *a lot* going on! If you are very empathetic, this might be the last place you want to spend your time because to sense all of that can be draining.

Many in this boat would consider themselves introverts. However, when you see these input as additional information and develop discernment of your center, the game magically changes! Others may not experience this particular sensitivity strongly. They likely have other latent superpowers that can be developed.

> *This is important because these additional senses begin to reveal the expanded realms of a fuller experience of the energy of Love.*

# CHAPTER 8

# Expansion Practices for Entry into the Heart

B y now, you understand a bigger picture of what Love is. It is the interpersonal human experience of care, affection, interaction, and connectedness. It is also who you are at the core of your being and your True Essence. This is the evolution: to marry the two levels of our experience as humans and spiritual beings. In previous chapters, you have been connecting to the Love around you and the Love that *is* you. It is time to deepen this connection.

These expanding exercises will help you bring this all into focus. There is also a new project – Tuning Your Energetic Heart. Through this project, you will experience new levels of self-integration. It represents a quantum leap in your evolution.

In addition, the Tuning to Your Physical Heart, Ceremony of Life Practice, and Unconditional Love practice build the machinery for the further evolutions of the heart and will aid your month-long project. Like all others in this book, these exercises develop your energetic, emotional, and physical muscles toward the wholeness of Love.

As always, consider engaging with these practices for at least four weeks before continuing.

## Practice Overview and Checklist

### Project

- Tuning Your Energetic Heart is a month-long project you will generate within yourself and create a physical representation for. It will utilize all the aspects you have established on your journey. This is a culmination of your learning and is akin to a thesis project for your pilgrimage back to self.

### Meditation

- Perform the root through solar plexus chanting exercise and finish by adding the heart chakra exercise detailed below for your meditation.
- After daily meditations, alternate using the new practices of Tuning to Your Physical Heart, and Unconditional Love.
- You are also welcome to revisit previous practices as daily meditation options.

### Journal

- Check in with your experience. Note any recent contractions, expansions, or questions that you may be reflecting on.
- Write about new experiences you have during new exercises.

## Tools to Practice Throughout Your Daily Life

You may notice that the list of practices has been culled to only your project and new exercises. The previous have all been building the foundation for the heart's octave.

- Tuning Your Energetic Heart*
- Everyday Ceremony of Life*

- Tuning to Your Physical Heart*
- The Practice of Unconditional Love*

*New practice

## Add to Your Meditation: Heart Chakra Humming

When working with the heart chakra, you work on themes of expanded Love. With clarity and balance, Love can flow from you to others and the universe and back into you with ease.

Perform regular daily meditation by readying your space, creating safety and comfort, breathwork, humming, and completing your practice through the solar plexus chakra.

Now add the heart chakra meditation while continuing to hum:

1. See in your mind's eye the sun's energy in your solar plexus buoyantly rising to the center of your chest in your heart chakra. Notice the energy moving up, becoming lighter. Then transforming into a beautiful emerald-green field of light. Feel the expansion of the energy as it moves into the heart space.

2. The beating of your heart is a symphony with all the other hearts in the universe. It communicates with the core of everything that exists and has ever existed. It is also what stores all your memories. Spend time in your heart and connect to remember. Absorb the information here. Tune into the frequency waves from all the hearts you create existence with.

3. Love is gravity. Love is re-uniting pieces of self and connecting with others. Feel the Love by imagining your heart shining in gold from the inside. If you look closer, the gold contains all the colors of the rainbow. Imagine these colors expanding out into the world, shining brightly.

4. Now, consciously generate a feeling of joy or Love in your heart. Feel that emotion move out through your right hand and into the world. Notice what your experience of this is.

5. Next, let the echo of that feeling reverberate back to you and come into your left hand. Allow your awareness sit back slightly as you allow the process to happen automatically. You are letting the heart do what it was designed to do. Start the circuit again and let it continually flow. Generating joy or Love, then letting it move out into the world to join the symphony of other hearts. Feel the energy come back to you.

6. Notice a tiny black speck in the center of your heart. It is so small that it is easy to miss. This tiny spot is the origin of the zero-point energy field and is a portal that connects back to the Creator. Move your awareness into this spot, feel the neutrality that exists here, and feel the access to your beingness beyond your human. The heart represents a place for both to exist simultaneously in this way. It is also where Unconditional and Universal Love exists, in a place of neutrality and connection.

7. Hold your awareness on both. You are a conduit of the divine in human form, and this is where you can connect with that truth. Spend some time in this place and just be.

8. As you feel the process come to completion, finish your practice as before. Keep your eyes closed and do a physical body scan with your hands, massaging and touching your body parts to ground yourself back in and create comfort within. If you feel pulled, sit with your experience and see if anything arises. Journal about anything you are drawn to further explore.

Pay special attention to the Tuning into your Energetic Heart Project, as this is a month-long project you will engage in to integrate themes in your life towards greater internal unity.

**Tuning Your Energetic Heart Project #1**

Going into your heart, you go back to your past, and the past gives meaning to the future. Recall the small dot, like the size of a pinhead, in your heart chakra that connects you to the source of creation. When you return to your heart, you can make sense of our soul's complete experience all the way back to the IAM.

*However, for this project, you will focus on integrating and tuning connections showing up in your current life. This can be accomplished in about a month.*

This exercise will be like a thesis project for our journey together. Start planning for it in the beginning of the month. You will create something like a map or web that connects the experiences in your heart from the now of your current incarnation.

You will utilize awareness, understanding, and feeling sensations. All the technologies we have been honing. Your five senses (sight, sound, taste, smell, touch), will then create something new through linking different aspects of your experience to a single node or point. This brings organization to your life experiences, by creating a tapestry of points that connects you into the web of your whole life. Your individual web can then be integrated into the larger web of life.

You can focus on one creative medium or use multiple as you are inspired to build and connect your points. You can paint, build, draw, cook, quilt—anything you can create with. It can even be a creation of a web that you build over time in your mind. Let yourself be drawn to the project, let it unfold, and be fun! Know that if you are feeling stifled or blocked, seek the place without mind to create. This exercise will be a balance of using thinking and not thinking (creating).

*You are beginning a deeper road to balancing the heart to create a balanced life. Heart harmony is needed to attract harmonious experiences. This harmony is what many people are actually seeking for their lives through spirituality*

You are ushering in a permanent coherence to the heart because you (and the collective) have forgotten your connection to everything. You have even forgotten the context for the parts of your experience from this incarnation. This project will help pull together these parts, integrate them in a balanced way, and show you how to continue the process.

Disconnection from the awareness and understanding of all the connections between yourself and others in the experiences in your life, often necessitates a crisis (an accident, sickness, breakup, or other difficulty) to create change in your life. This can lead to quicker change but can also create suffering.

*Suffering happens because when change is quick, your heart has not yet caught up with the difference between states before and after. The more significant the difference in these states, the greater the potential suffering.*

You will learn and practice how to "tune" yourself to integrate your life experiences. This month will focus on the situations in your present life.

*At each of the following steps, recognize that you are the center of your experience (I AM).*

### Step 1: Awareness

You can start by asking yourself what is happening now in your life. Seek awareness of both the positive and the negative aspects of what you are experiencing. The negative reflections can be more challenging to understand when there is a "charge." Defuse the charge by finding your center, seeing a drama triangle, and practicing forgiveness.

What is difficult between you and others? What is being reflected to you by people or situations in your job, family, friends, etc.? If you don't know where to start, you can either start with the struggles and successes that are more obvious or section your self-inquiry into areas to focus on for a week (career, partnership, family, health, etc.). If you engage the latter method, I suggest choosing three and leaving the fourth week for deeper integration of the whole project.

Sometimes, situations are a mix of polarity where some aspects are challenging, and others are uplifting or effortless. Focus on one situation at a time, and in this step, you aim to understand all the parts. It takes practice and a certain emotional maturity to seek these themes earnestly.

> *You are looking for all the reflections in your life. The reflections are what you perceive in someone else and in situations that arise.*

For example, if you perceive your boss to be selfish, seek where you may be selfish in your life. Your boss may indeed be selfish, but this is about what they are reflecting to you. They are part of the network of reality and have a gift for you if you are ready to receive it. Anywhere in your life where someone or something triggers you is a reflection of yourself. Seeing the reflections can be the most challenging part.

Once you move through all the steps, you will show up differently in these situations. The energy between you will not be the same. Regarding the example above, the fact that your boss is selfish will no longer agitate you. You will be able to hold space for their separate human experience.

### Step 2: Connect
In this step, you will make the connection between what you learned about yourself from Step 1 and illuminate where this theme has come up before in your life. Sticking with our previous example, maybe you

have commonly said or thought in the past, "Why do selfish people always surround me?" or "All I do is give, and selfish people around me just take."

The dynamic could be different for individual situations here. In this example, you would consider why you give more than you are actually comfortable giving. This is related to a solar plexus theme of not being in the center of yourself or fully being the center of your reality. Many of the reflections you will uncover will be about solar plexus imbalances. Although, themes may arise from any of the chakras we have covered. Through this practice, you define who you are in relation to others in your reality.

Step 2 is a great time to use meditation. You can set an intention for more understanding about a specific theme you are working on before the meditation (feel the desire for understanding in your heart), meditate to open yourself, and then spend some time at the end with the openness you created for new perspectives to come in. Use parts of our established meditation practice – readying yourself, creating safety, breathwork, and closing the practice.

Another alternative is using a creative outlet to access the right brain and receive insights. Some people already enjoy creative outlets, others have always wanted a creative outlet but have not made time for it, and some are not drawn at all. Use your intuition and follow what you would Love. Engage your creativity in the way you are called to.

Use your creative outlet much like you would meditation. Set your intention, let it go, make your creations, and then remain open for insights.

You may find some juicy patterns that have been with you for decades and can be difficult to see clearly. Take your time with these more ingrained patterns and let them marinate. You can move to another one as you will still be subconsciously "chewing" on the previous one.

Each situation you identify will constitute a point in your web. Make sure to journal about your insights as a method to process situations and document them. Then you will use the information to create new web points.

### Step 3: Feel & Integrate

In this step, we will integrate insights from the previous step through meditation. Use the full chakra humming meditation to integrate the understanding into the fullness of your being. Start as you have before through all the step and the four chakras. Then with your awareness still in your heart, feel the emotions and sensations you generated for a node identified in Step 2. Take this feeling back to the Creator in the zero-point energy spot in the center of your heart.

> *The most important part of this step is first to feel the sensations in your body that come up around the theme you have identified. Locate the sensation and where it is in your body. Then, bring it back to the deepest place in your heart to be integrated.*

Repeat the practice for each point. Consider giving each node its own day, or a separate time when starting out. When you become more proficient, maybe you can integrate a few in the same meditation. At the same time, remembering that there is no rush.

Journal about your experience and each point that you are uncovering and integrating.

### Step 4: Create Your Web

Next, you will take all the points you have found during previous steps and, without your thinking mind, organize them in a creative representation. What is creating? It is connecting what already exists to produce something new. You are always using the poles to create something new.

What you have been doing throughout the steps of this project is balancing internal polarity and creating something new within yourself. Now, you will take the integrated pieces and organize them using less thinking mind and more intuition. There is no need to judge any of it. This does not need to be the most beautiful piece of art.

At this step, each point you create is a connective nexus that represents the Love and beauty from your life's experience and growth. These points represent both poles and the integration of those poles to balance.

The materials you use to create can be anything. It can be as extravagant or simple as you want. This project is for you and you only. Check in and remember that you are the center of your experience.

Here are some ideas: painting, making a collage, drawing, cooking, building something, writing a story where each node is a character/archetype (not the story of your life), knitting, or rearranging your house. This is not an exhaustive list and leave room for your own inspiration.

If you are struggling to find the right medium, keep it simple. A pen and a piece of paper will work fine. It is possible to create the web entirely in your mind also if you are drawn to do this.

Ask yourself how does the energy want to be created and connected? The sooner you get started, the faster you will find an intuitive flow for the project. Take each small step, and you will see the next one. When you get into the flow of connecting the points, you will receive further insights. There are metaphors here about the larger design of your life. Notice them and document them in your journal.

This is a big project, and I invite you to feel into how long you need. Four weeks may not be enough for this first phase, which is ok. There is no hurry; it is not a race. It is an experience! You could spend a year on this initial project or a lifetime. Everyone will get there in their own time.

Remember, change that is too quick without having time to tune the heart can bring suffering. You are precisely where you need to be. You are only focusing on the connections from the now of your experience. When you become a master of this phase, you will continue the practice, potentially in the following month.

Next, check out your additional practices for the month. As always, add these to your daily rotation. Becoming adept at utilizing them at the end of meditations and applying them to your daily life is very important. First, you will get acquainted with practices and perspectives that *tune* you into your physical heart.

## Tuning to Your Physical Heart

The beating of your heart keeps you alive, circulates hormones and many other healing molecules, sends/receives information throughout your world and the cosmos, and records all your experiences. What an incredible organ! Yet, how well do you know the beating of your heart? This practice aims to help you develop a deeper relationship with your physical heart. This will bring awareness as you go through your day when your heart beats faster (excitement or stress) and beats more slowly (calm or relaxed).

Have you ever heard your own heartbeat? You may have felt it in your neck or wrist by placing your fingers on an artery there and feeling the pulse of blood as it was pumped. You can feel your heartbeat when you place a hand on your chest. Some people can hear their heartbeat when they cover their ears with the heel of their hand.

Most need a device like a stethoscope, or even some apps claim to record heartbeat audio. You can have a loved one put their head on your chest, listen, and tell you what it sounds like. In some way, get to know the beat and rhythm of your heart.

Similar to how a cat's meow sounds different according to particular languages (ex. "meow" in English, "mew" in Welsh, and "meong" in Indonesian), what is the language of your heart? Is it a lub-dub, bum-bum, or ba-bump? Decipher this sound for yourself, paying attention to the two separate sounds of expansion and contraction.

Start to get to know your physical heart by tuning into it on all these levels. Make this a practice before your sleep, when you wake up, meditate, or throughout your day. Acknowledge your heart and all its practical roles and energetic aspects.

Then, move deeper. With your hand on your chest, imagine feeling excitement. You may need to connect with a past experience to conjure the feeling. Notice how your heart speeds up and what that feels like. Know that pumping hormones match this feeling to every corner of your body.

Next, imagine a feeling of calm. You can bring on the feeling by imagining spending time with a pet or loved one. Maybe imagining yourself on a tropical beach will do it. Observe how your heart responds. Connect this feeling with the totality of what the heart is for your experience.

You create coherence between the mind and heart by getting to know your heart. Coherence means more resilience, health, and self-awareness.

Get to know the following practice, Everyday Ceremony of Life.

## Everyday Ceremony of Life

A ceremony is an activity done with a feeling of reverence in a sacred space. Your intention, presence, awareness, and consciousness all create this. You can make anything you do a sacred experience because, in truth, every moment and creation is already sacred. You are simply tuning to it. It is your awareness of that fact, coupled with intention, hooks us into the essence of that moment in a special way.

I invite you to make this a daily "walking" meditation practice. Anything you do can be a ceremony. The meditation practice you have been cultivating is already a daily ceremony you have made a habit. Don't let the feeling of familiarity with a task, process, or thing take you out of the sacredness right before you.

In your day-to-day life, approach tasks with this level of focus. Maybe you turn washing the dishes into a sacred act. The more mundane the task, the better to start! It is fun to incorporate the senses in this—for example, smelling a rose and experiencing the beauty and the intoxicating fragrance with intention, presence, and awareness.

Because you are fully aware and present with the activity in this sacred place, you are aware of your emotions/thoughts and can tune as you go. Tune to what is before you in the moment and bring the information back to your heart in the zero-point-energy field.

The universe is always mirroring something back to you, so when you literally stop to smell a rose with a ceremonial presence, the rose will have a message for you. Tune in to intuit a feeling, image, or other message. This is possible with all that you encounter.

I have observed this phenomenon clearly with ceremonial cacao. You can drink sacred chocolate with intention and feel the expansion and depth of reality. It opens your heart space and helps you connect with yourself and the world. This leads to intuition and guidance. However, if you drink ceremonial cacao without intention, presence, and awareness, you will not be able to hear the messages it has for you.

You can create a similar experience on your own in a meditative space. Throughout this book, you have worked your muscles of awareness, intention, and presence. Now, bring them together to experience the profound within the mundane. It is there if you know how to listen to it.

This practice does not have to take much time, though it may be fun to play with staying in this state for more extended periods. Engage some of your regular five senses, then go beyond them to the expanded space around you. Bring in and apply all your learnings from your journey. Enjoy the awareness and excitement as your life reflects how magical being alive is!

Journal about your experiences bringing the sacred to the mundane as you continue to master this practice.

Next is the Practice of Unconditional Love.

## The Practice of Unconditional Love

As introduced in chapter 7, *Unconditional Love* can be defined as loving all that is without the need to change it.

Let's go back through the "Meet Love in Multiple Contexts" section from this expanded perspective of Love. Here is a meditation to help invite the perspective in. If you get stuck on whether what you are seeing is real or not, just know that it does not matter. The visualization helps bring concepts in somatically by accessing the right brain. It is based on a meditation by Dr. Julia Mossbridge, a researcher of Unconditional Love.

You can engage the meditation preparation steps as you have many times before.

1. Then close your eyes and get comfortable either in a seated tetrahedral position or lying down.

2. Imagine a tree coming up from the center of the Earth that reaches up to connect with your tailbone. This is your grounding cord that allows bidirectional energy. Energy can come up from the Earth, and any energy that you don't need can move back down to be recycled.

3. Next, imagine a golden orb of light above your head. This is your own sun and the Unconditional Love from the universe made explicitly for you and through you. It has frequencies tuned to your specific soul. Does it sparkle? Can you see beams of light radiating from it? The golden light beams from that orb down to the top of your head and inside your brain. It then travels down your nervous system and out to all your organs. Watch it radiate down to your feet and find its way into your body's tissues until it permeates the whole thing.

4. Next, put the light in the area around your body in the shape of an egg. There is an unending source of this golden Unconditional Love that completely fills you up. Realize that this is readily available to you at any time. You are simply connecting to something that is already there.

5. Go through the description of all the love types and experience them from this place—notice and journal about your practice.

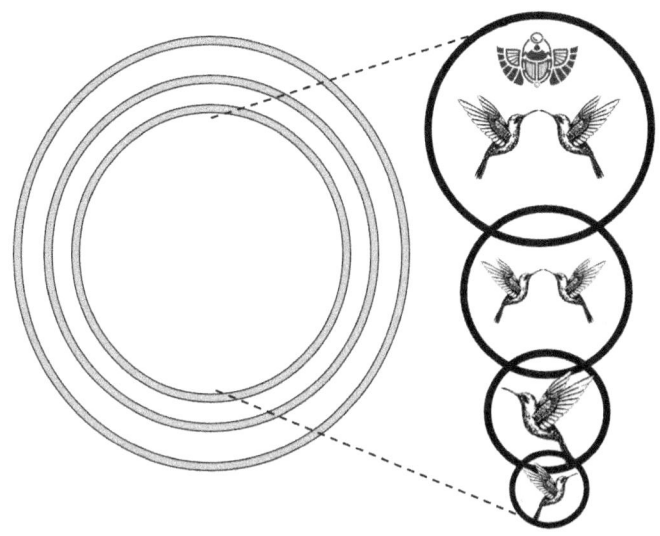

# Deeper into the Fourth Octave:
# Chapters 9 and 10

## Expanded Heart (Astral Plane)

Love is the vibration and gravity of creation.

***Old Perspective:*** *An unconscious belief that "I am limited and need to expand to escape my human experience."*

***New Perspective:*** *A conscious awareness, as in "I AM already."*

CHAPTER 9:

# Love Manifests Form

*Creativity is just intelligence having fun!*

—Albert Einstein

Love is the energy and gravity between each pole. It magnetically brings union in opposing poles throughout every level of existence. Love is that which creates all that is new and is between all that is created. Love manifests form.

For this book, I would amend Einstein's above quote to *"All creation is just intelligence having fun!"* All levels of creation, from God to a cell dividing in you or a plant, are the intelligent conscious fields enjoying the creation process. This is Love, whether it is you creating or a bigger or smaller force in existence.

Given the average level of consciousness currently on the planet, much of creation still occurs from unbalanced separate selves. Imbalanced creation occurs from this separation through the seeking of self in others and is not a representation of creation from the True Self. Then, only the needs of the individual or small group of individuals influence the creation from *lack, scarcity,* or *inadequacy.* This limits our world significantly. Creation can occur with and through the force of spirit, elevating all that is formed, shaped, and built.

This book's perspectives and exercises have been geared distilling you down to your True Self. This serves as a giant leap that many have stopped short of reaching. It represents the potential union of both brain hemispheres and the union within the self. This is the union of your internal polarity.

The essence of this can be found in any union, such as your merging with nature or with a romantic partner. It also exists in the union of protons and neutrons in the nucleus of all atoms, in electrons between molecules, and in the reproduction of cells or animals. It is the process of union within all things. Therefore, the drive towards union exists within, between, the "above and below," and even through it all!

> *The secret in this chapter is that Love manifests form through union at every level of existence. Love is part of a gravitational and magnetic force, bringing two parts together to make a whole. This process applies to magnetizing the expanded parts of the self also, leading to further spiritual evolution.*

When you connect with something greater than yourself, you move closer to the essence of wholeness. This is also a conduit to God, the Creator of all. In this state, you also connect with the true nature of yourself beyond this human experience. You manifest from divine will when you create your perspectives and world from a place of internal unity. There is so much joy, connection, and Love available here!

When you unite the ways of logic with the ways of intuition, you can access the heart's intelligence, as established in chapter 7. Then, personality begins to integrate its separate parts and becomes whole. Here, a new state of consciousness is born. Synchronicities abound in this place as a new flow enters your experience, and inner harmony permeates your life.

Not being in this state creates a life where there is a need to be completed by something external, such as a partner, material accumulation, or success. When you are integrated, the answer to the need always comes from within. This is when aligned manifestation starts to come online. Union, in partnership with another, can also bring you to higher states. If this is of interest, see Sovatsky's *Advanced Spiritual Intimacy.*

Union of self is what we are pointing to. One can further nurture this burgeoning inner state by consciously balancing your personality's inner masculine and feminine aspects. We all have a mixture of masculine and feminine traits and natural tendencies, regardless of sex or gender. These make up your individual personality.

You may naturally have a more passionate and fiery temperament, which tends to be a more masculine trait, exemplifying impulsiveness, eagerness, fierceness, and drive. Female characteristics are more careful, calm, and settled, and there is a "holding" nature to this energy. Once you have obtained a balanced state of the poles within yourself, you must practice and maintain your internal presence. This means you sustain your balance no matter what is occurring in your external world.

This centered state has been cultivated since chapter 5's discussion on the solar plexus. By keeping a centered state, you connect with your internal source of talent and intuition. In the expansion practices chapter that follows, you will create a deeper space to hold this balance and bring in higher elements of yourself through your Inner Heart Union Ceremony, the culmination of this book.

# Further Opening to the Sacred

There is a point where words struggle to describe the processes within us or the universe adequately. This is the realm of the sacred. The left brain cannot access or understand this realm as, in fact, it is not meant to be understood through language and analysis. It is intended to be experienced through right-brained observation and somatic emotions.

Throughout this book, groundwork has been laid to access more felt emotions to aid progress in your final evolutions. Chapter 1 connected hormones and emotions to behavior, and chapter 3 described a link between the creation of health in the body and an expanded experience of your reality. Throughout our journey with the feelings and emotions that you are cultivating, you may have already experienced things that are difficult to put into words.

This is not about expanded experiences that are brought on by psychedelics. This describes an expanded awareness of the world with only the substances your body makes. Psychedelic use has skyrocketed in the last few years.

In my perspective, it has a place in our evolution because the human species has been stuck in ways of being that no longer serve us. Psychedelics can show the user what is possible when they fully utilize the technology of their human form. However, these states can be experienced entirely without substance through your cultivated hormones.

I am pointing to that path; everything you need is already inside you. You can access an expanded experience at any moment. It is just expanding your awareness. This is why ritual or practice has been so powerful for thousands of years. When you create a practice or engage in a ritual, you focus all your awareness and presence on that activity. When you are not present, your awareness is diffuse, making it easy to go unconscious.

For example, when you are meditating, the activity of emptying your mind is all that exists. You are creating space to be as present as possible, focusing your awareness, and moving into a right-brain-dominated perception. You can take this a step further and practice it during everyday life. The Everyday Ceremony of Life practice in the previous chapter has introduced this to you. Then in the following expanded practices chapter, practicing The Feeling of Oneness will help your continued cultivation.

When you open yourself to the dimension where everything is sacred, you'll experience reverence and joy *in* and *for* everything you do. This is the practice of expanding your experience. Having mastery over this can't be undervalued! When you meet life in this way, you can begin to see all the information reflecting back to you at any moment. This practice cultivates a sense of awe for all experiences of life.

## Union and the Mysteries

Self-union is the merging of the poles, opposites, or masculine and feminine energies within the self, but it can also occur in union with another. This is part of our experience as humans that utilize polarity for creating matter to continue ourselves. It is observed during the conception of children, although creation energy always occurs when poles come together. This can be a permanent fusion of two becoming one or an experience of oneness that forever changes the individual components.

Hormones and connection are ways to experience union as part of human technology. This is a simple introduction to a vast topic that straddles Kundalini and the ways of the Tao that are beyond the scope of this book. What is important here is that you begin to understand and connect with union in multiple forms. Where you put your awareness with perspective is very powerful and can open up worlds of experience.

This brings awareness to the union cultivated within you so you can commune more deeply with others and the world around you.

## Worship as a Sacred Act

Continuing in the realm of the sacred, let's consider the idea of worship in our approach to union. In his book *Advanced Spiritual Intimacy*, Stuart Sovatsky writes:

> Worship is what even the immortals long to do, and they willingly relinquish their immortality in order to find something to bow to. What they long to worship is the other, not themselves. Thus, the immortals become the other—that is, mortals—in order to carry out their sacred rites. They become us, we become them, over and over again.

This is the crux of the magnetism between humans in romantic pair-bonding from the spiritual perspective. Before incarnating into this human experience, your soul has and is everything already. We come here to relinquish all and forget what we had, to experience the drive toward "that" again. This is the separation into poles (separate from spirit into human) to have an experience of reuniting with that pole again.

What "that" is enters the realm of the sacred. This signals the need to access it through a higher frequency of feeling. In the case of union, worship is the vehicle back to the immortal. I interpret "immortal" as referring to when we are in spiritual form, not human form. Awe and devotion are also related to the experience of worship. When union occurs through worship, a connection rings down to the depths of our beingness and triggers a remembering of the immortal. Activating worship for the other is what opens this up.

Once you realize you are more than human and that your deepest cravings cannot be met by the mundane, this is what we receive.

This craving to return to our true nature drives many to understand themselves and their reality more deeply.

Then, it is through worship and devotion to the other—which can be a partner, higher parts of self, God, or an aspect of nature—that we can experience the divine between ourselves and all these levels. Through devotion to the other, you are pulled toward a complementary facet to glimpse a reflection of what you knew before your human incarnation when you were immortal and spirit. The process of remembering.

*Worship seeks the beloved for union through the greater aspects of Love.*

## Manifesting (Creating) from a Balanced Heart

The prevalence of the term manifesting has grown in pop spiritualism for the last few decades. However, as discussed previously, the level of consciousness doing the manifesting sets the frequency level of the practice's capabilities. As the idea of manifesting has been popularized, it seems used chiefly to manifest things people *think* they want.

This is manifesting from the unbalanced separate self. Remember, this is the part of the self that thinks it is not whole on its own. You *need* that thing because you are in a state of lack. This is what happens when you fall in love with something that is not in your highest good. Need will always create more need in this way.

By balancing the separate self, the place from which you manifest will begin to shift. Initially, it is suggested not to manifesting specific things like a car, a job title, or a house. Instead, manifest the feelings you want to feel.

Most people would like to feel more joy, happiness, and fulfillment. Manifest the feeling! Feel it in your body. The secret is to fall in Love with it, feel your gravity pull it to you, and attract that possibility. Then, let the spirit decide how exactly it should happen.

When you leave room for this collaboration, things beyond your wildest dreams will occur! This is falling in Unconditional Love with a reality you want to create. Meaning you are open to when that reality needs you and not the other way around.

> *Remember that your heart is always manifesting your reality from the frequencies you are generating from your heart. Awareness is needed to observe where you are unconsciously and consciously manifesting from. Align these two.*

When manifesting comes from the simplistic nature of only the human, it immediately limits itself. As you evolve your manifestation practice and continue to balance your heart, your abilities increase to create your reality. It is like we unlock a certain level of frequency, where we have earned a new level of responsibility that opens your access to a broader playground.

This is because the quality and level of frequency with which you create your reality determine the depth of how fulfilling your creations are.

> *Evolution is the interplay between habit and creativity.*
>
> —Rupert Sheldrake

Your continued evolution from this point on will be the intelligence and creativity you bring to this human experience *with* the spirit of evolution. You should now fully embody that you are no longer simply a human but a soul having a human experience. As you move through the expansion practices, this will blossom more fully if you show the universe that you can manifest your reality in alignment with it.

# Intuition

As I have mentioned before, everyone reading this book has experienced intuition in their lives at some time. I have waited to give some basic guidance on the topic because if you have done the practices earnestly, you will notice your intuition has opened more already. Furthermore, your ability to listen to these extra senses should be heightened.

The discussion becomes simpler, as the mind is more open to letting information in. You may even begin to experience the opening of somatic intuitive tells, such as tingling feelings, an excitement in the heart, or other senses when you are being guided. Realize that these five expanded senses exist beyond your human brain and accesses more of reality. As a spiritual being without a body, you have only these intuitive senses through which you perceive and move about the universe. As a human being, you are simply remembering this.

The continued development of your intuitive muscle is the awareness that you have had these experiences all along and that they are innate. Meeting these experiences from this open place will help you more easily realize when you have them and create a relationship with this expanded part of yourself.

The second step in developing your intuition is creating more access to the right side of your brain, which you have already spent much time cultivating throughout this book. This allows this side of your brain to access your heart's intelligence and bring your intuition online. Becoming aware of when you have an intuition is key. This helps you learn to trust the information through acknowledgment.

Next, let's bring further understanding the five claire-senses to better understand when and how information may come through:

- *Claircognizance* can feel like a knowing was just dropped into your brain. It literally translates to "clear knowing."
- *Clairvoyance* is "clear seeing" and is experienced via visions with your eyes open or images with your eyes closed.
- *Clairsentience* is when you have increased empathy for emotions and energies around you. This word translates to "clear feeling."
- *Clairalience* and *clairgustance* is where you have phantom smells and tastes, respectively.

You likely have an affinity for at least one of these expanded senses, usually claircognizance, clairvoyance, or clairsentience. It is useful to identify which comes easiest to you and the ones that you would like to develop further.

## Chapter Recap

### Illuminated Takeaway

*You are at the threshold of a more profound knowing and being in yourself. This deeper activation further embodies your soul, the truth of who you are, and your individual spiritual gifts.*

Whereas chapters 7 and 8 had goals of clearing and activating the heart space, each of the newly introduced practices in chapter 10 are designed to expand this to the realm of your spiritual nature. As mentioned in the heart chakra description, this chakra is the border between the more expanded spiritual chakras and has aspects of both the human and the spirit. The invitation in this chapter opens the doorway to increased balance between the human and spiritual aspects of self.

This may have been the shortest chapter, but it is the most profound. All the essential work to reach this crescendo has been accomplished, and now applying further expansions and principles becomes easier. Leave space to continue to experience your own evolution alongside all the creative forces; the play (work) now becomes fully your experience as you move deeper and deeper towards union. Engage with your final expansion practices chapter with reverence and sacred space.

**At this point in your journey, you may begin to experience . . .**

- New perspectives about the totality of what Love really is and how it permeates your life
- A curiosity about how the unification of two creates and what you experience if you tune to the sacredness there
- An awareness of the masculine and feminine principles through which you create your reality
- A spark of connection with the subtle field of the creation of spirit, which is waiting to collaborate with you

# CHAPTER 10

# Expansion Practices for the Expanded Heart

C hapter 9 took a sharp shift to point to the sacred concepts and mysteries that cannot be fully understood, only experienced. With the previous expansion practices, you've developed expanded feelings of gratitude, different types of Love, admiration, and forgiveness—all as a portal to a growing felt understanding of unity. This unity exists already within and throughout all we are remembering.

The exercises in this chapter are where you can continue to develop access to these expanded places and feelings. This opens your human technology up to remembering experiences before this incarnation and is the marriage between the human and the divine self. Here are your final expansion practices in our journey together.

At this point in your journey, you'll begin to experience:

- A new feeling of unfolding and opening in your awareness through the understanding of the fullness of Love

- A continued feeling of your physical awareness expanding in your body
- A sense of creating with the universe and the universe creating through you

Please consider practicing the new exercises daily for a minimum of four weeks.

# Practice Overview and Checklist

## Project

- Continue the project you started in chapter 8. You will focus on other phases of your life and add to your already created physical representation.

## Meditation

- Practice your new chakra toning exercise, introduced below, two or three times weekly through the month.
- Focus on the practicing The Feeling of Oneness at the end of meditations and throughout your day. Leaving the Inner Heart Union Ceremony as its own event. You may continue integrating other practices from previous chapters as internally guided.
- On or around day 30, you will perform your Inner Heart Ceremony.

## Journal

- Check in with your experience. Note any recent contractions, expansions, or questions that you may be reflecting on.
- Moment of expansion: Can you feel the omnipresence of Love waiting to connect with you more deeply?

## Tools to Practice Throughout Your Daily Life

Focus on the new practices, and all will culminate in the Inner Heart Union Ceremony. Feel free to use some of the previous chapter's practices if you are guided.

- Tuning Your Energetic Heart #2*
- The Feeling of Oneness*
- Inner Heart Union Ceremony*

*New practice

## Tuning Your Energetic Heart #2

In the previous practices chapter, we introduced this project and focused on integrating the self from the perspective of what is happening in your life now. Next, we will expand the focus to include how these patterns of the present connect with other phases of your life. During last month's process, you may have noticed larger patterns coming up to be connected and included them in your project. Now, you will focus more on these connections.

First, identify how you want to organize the phases of your life. It could be childhood, adolescence, adulthood, and the present (the previous chapter's focus). You are welcome to choose other ways of organizing it. It will be helpful to choose three and dedicate a week to each. Then, you can leave the last week for creating and integration. It may be easiest to start with the most recent phase, as phases always dip into previous phases. This is because we are illuminating patterns that often began at previous times.

One strategy is to use the previously identified points to follow the thread to older phases. Then complete the links between and the entire path of that one theme. It is important to take this in phases because it will give you a different perspective to put your mind and emotions in your experience at different ages. This is an excellent strategy to start with that may illuminate other points in your web.

You are piecing it out and staying out of the story as much as possible. The story you have been telling yourself about who you are and what others and life have "done" to you has limited you. The IAM and the center of your experience is who you are.

*This project is reorganizing all the information to be in coherence with the evolution you are experiencing.*

As you start exploring the next phase, ask yourself these questions:

- Who were the prominent people around me at this time in my life?
- What were my most difficult situations or learnings during this phase?
- What feelings did I feel daily?
-  What feelings did I deny daily?
- What were the mechanisms I used to cope with denied feelings?

You are bringing yourself back to a previous phase. Now you can "work" the steps as you did before:

- Step 1: Awareness
- Step 2: Connect
- Step 3: Integrate
- Step 4: Continue Creating Your Web

   (More details on each step in chapter 8)

As before, take your time with this. If it takes more than four weeks, that is ok. What is important is that you are learning how to keep coming back to your heart to integrate your experience. Then you can better understand the polarity you will continue to create with throughout your life. You now have new understandings and tools to live from the expanded perspective of how it is all connected to you, and you are all connected to it.

Remember, this project is helping you repeatedly bring yourself back to your heart to tune the polarities of your experience. If you have a big contracting emotion, practice returning this energy to your heart. It is the same if you have a considerable expanding experience- return to the heart and use the tuning process through the zero-point energy field.

Why do we need to tune expanding experiences? Because polarity always exists. When you move strongly towards one pole, the other will quickly follow! When there is not a balancing, this can be very jarring. To tune is to balance. To have a balanced heart is to have a life of harmony.

Recall the polarity of the beating (bum-bum) of your heart. From a heart perspective, the ultimate balance would be constantly tuning the frequencies of the emotions going out and coming in. When you return to the heart and give meaning to everything in your life, you can begin transforming it. Keep these themes of the heart in mind as you continue.

*Return to your heart often! Tuning to your heart also means seeking guidance inside for everything in your life. Your heart always knows.*

Work becomes play when you live in tune with your heart. Everything about your life suddenly becomes enjoyable. Your creatorship is in this realm of play and enjoyment. You can continue tuning yourself to this space by doing more things you enjoy and creating laughter daily.

After practicing connecting the points for your present and past experiences from this life, you are ready for your Inner Heart Union Ceremony. It will be far more impactful if the work has been done earnestly. At the same time, it does not need to be perfect! You will know when you feel a sense of accomplishment and your intuition tells you it is time.

## Meditation with Chakra Toning (Two or Three Times Weekly)

Introduced here is a similar meditation practice but using sound to prepare the chakras for your Inner Heart Ceremony at the end of the month. At this point, you are well versed with the different emotional concepts in each chakra and have been working to tune in to them based on these concepts. Now, we introduce vowel toning to gain deeper access to chakra activations. Vowel toning is an ancient practice that strengthens the body's energy centers.

1. Start your practice as before by readying your space, creating safety and comfort, adding breathwork, and humming.

2. Verbally set your intentions before this practice. Here is an example: *With my I AM presence, I engage in this practice to open and expand my chakras to the greatest and highest good available. I ask that anything that no longer aligns with my mind, body, or emotions be transmuted in the highest way possible to the extent that I am currently available to process comfortably.*

3. Move your awareness up to your root chakra. Take a deep breath through your nose and make the sound *uhh* for a full breath. Then, repeat seven times.

4. Now, move up to your sacral chakra. Take a deep breath through your nose and make the sound *ooo* for a full breath. Repeat seven more times.

5. Then, bring your awareness up to the solar plexus chakra. Take a deep breath through your nose and make the sound *ohh* for a full breath. Repeat seven more times.

6. Next, move up to your heart chakra space. Take a deep breath through your nose and make the sound *ahh* for a full breath. Repeat seven times.

7. As you feel the process come to completion, finish your practice. Keep your eyes closed and do a physical body scan with your hands, massaging and touching your body parts to ground yourself back in the body and create comfort within. Linger here for as long as it feels good. Journal about your experience or anything that arises.

## The Feeling of Oneness

Purposefully experiencing a feeling of oneness helps open us to the connection between all things. This can be done by seeing and connecting with your own godliness and then seeing and connecting with the godliness of others. It is such a fun practice and offers an opportunity to feel a deep safety with others, even strangers. Start by getting to know the exercise as a meditation, then practice it out in the world. Here are the steps:

1. Perform each meditation practice step: readying yourself, creating safety and comfort, breathwork, humming, and/or watching the thinker.

2. Take a bit of your consciousness down to your heart space and imagine a brightly shining golden light there, emanating from the zero-point energy dot. When you find it, what does that light feel like? Is it warm and inviting? Does it feel safe, relaxing, or peaceful? Spend a moment with these feelings.

3. Know that this is your soul light. This is one of the places that light enters your body and is one of your direct connections to

God. It is here that, in the moments in between breaths, God initiates each breath you have. The Creator is always with you and *is* you. The energy that animates you and the material of your soul has come here to have a three-dimensional experience. You are God having a human experience.

4. The cool thing about your being God is that everyone and everything else is also God separated, having a different experience and perspective. What is it like to look at the world through this felt perspective? I have had amazingly connected experiences with animals and humans while in this place. As you start to operate from this space, it creates safety with your surroundings. This occurs because your state sends a signal that I am you and you are me. Which to the beings you encounter is an awareness of a connection that feels to the subconscious like *That person wouldn't hurt me, just like I would not hurt myself.*

5. If in meditation, close your practice as you have each time before.

Next, to take it out into the world! Practice this anywhere, even with strangers at the grocery store. First, find your golden light and your godliness. Then, in your mind, say, "I am God, and I see that you are also God," while you are around strangers. This is a fascinating practice because you may feel different reactions. Some will not want to see you as God subconsciously, and some will not want to see themselves as God. If you pick up on this subtlety, just reply in your mind, "It's okay; I still see that I am God and that you are also God." This is fun to do with your pets and other animals in the wild.

The more you use this practice, the more you create safety within yourself and in the world around you. This opens the door to oneness consciousness and expanded levels of the heart chakra.

Continue to practice your mediations and additional practices for about a month or when you are guided. Then ready yourself for your Inner Heart Union Ceremony!

## Day 30: The Inner Heart Union Ceremony

Do the other practices for four weeks and leave this as a one-event practice at the end.

At this point in our journey, you have a solid foundation of flexibility in the mind and access to the heart space. Now that you are free of much of the density you have carried in your lifetime, you have created space to merge with your inner self. This Inner Heart Union Ceremony will help "seal in" all your accomplishments.

Beyond that, it invites a new level of higher consciousness to your experience that will continue to grow and expand. This new level will unify the two halves to create something new—the evolution of the parts that came together. This is an act of Love through a force of Love.

In this way, unification sets yet another foundation for further expansion through the additional chakras you can continue to explore beyond this book.

Here are the steps for your Inner Heart Union Ceremony:

1. Intuitively choose a day, time, and place that has meaning to you. You can consider astrology, phases of the moon, or upcoming seasonal markers as potent times for this ceremony. It can take place either outside or inside.

2. Update your sacred space. Pull together items that have significance or make you feel good to decorate your ceremonial space. Think about all the senses. Consider gathering essential

oils, incense, music, candles, blankets, clothing you feel comfortable in, flowers, or anything else you would like to use.

3. At your chosen time near your sacred space, you can smudge, burn incense, or use essential oils to clear yourself and your space.

4. Then, set your intent for complete internal union and a deepening of your soul's incarnation into your heart space. This occurs through an intense desire for this union, begin to feel this now.

5. Enter the space you created with reverence, presence, excitement, and this desire. Sit comfortably in your tetrahedral position and begin your usual meditation, readying yourself, creating safety and comfort, breathwork, humming, and toning through the heart chakra.

6. When finished, sit quietly, and feel the openness and expansion of all your first four chakras. Feel how ready you truly are! Then, focus all your attention on your heart space. Imagine a chamber there filled with rose-colored light—or any other color light your intuition guides you to perceive.

7. Ask out loud that all aspects of yourself—fragmented, separated, or not present and integrated—be washed by white light and returned to your heart space. Ask for this from all dimensions, past lives, timelines, spaces, and throughout time. You don't need to know the story about these different aspects you have been separated from. Just feel these pieces of you integrate back where they belong. Feel grateful for this reunion. Stay here for as long as the process takes to unfold before continuing to the next step.

8. Now focus your attention on your beloved, a great Love that you have for the higher aspects of yourself—the ray of light of your soul that condenses into form and who you indeed

are. Feel worship for this beloved aspect of self. This light contains information of endless wisdom, knowledge, and Love. Sense its radiant presence, enter your heart space, and take residence within the colored light. This presence brings with it an alchemical change that unifies with you. You may experience a feeling of lightness, bliss, and of coming home.

9. Whatever was left in a previous frequency is brought up to match your new higher self. Watch or feel the dissolving of self into Self as your heart continues to lighten. Connect with the relief that these higher aspects are there to support you, offering higher wisdom, your Loving internal guide, and your upgraded connection to your beingness.

10. Stay in this place for as long as possible and visit it frequently throughout the day. This will assist in the unfolding and strengthening of unification. The more time spent here, the greater and more significant the effect. When not in that space, check-in and recognize the pink glow radiating from your heart chakra. Experience the peace, warmth, and contentment that the glow offers as it integrates and penetrates each cell of your body over time. Completing this process varies from person to person, so make communing in this place part of your daily meditations.

As full integration of your higher aspect occurs, our intuition increases further. If you can hear your intuition, the voice may change and get stronger with time, your knowings may become more apparent, and your empathy may get a boost. If you did not previously have access to one of the clair-senses, a new one may open to you. Play with feeling this oneness within yourself and how that oneness extends to all that is. Within this web, you remember more of who you are in the cosmos.

Old patterns may still emerge as the process unfolds. Hold your connection to the chamber you created within your heart and utilize one of the many tools you have learned through the expansion practices. In the beginning, you may find that you need to be around people who are easier to get along with. It may feel like the unconsciousness of others brings you out of communion, but this is not permanent.

You may need to create some space for yourself as you better understand the new territory you have entered. You are still developing and understanding this new union, which is akin to a second childhood. Journaling about your experience through the ceremony and afterward can be very helpful. Keeping track of your progress can assist to know when a new phase of stability has come in.

# CHAPTER 11

# Concluding Our Journey Begins Another

## Check-In with Where You Are Now

Take a moment to feel a sense of accomplishment for whatever advancement you experienced during our time together. Remember, your only goal is the experience of the journey and not a destination. Spend some time reflecting on how you have grown throughout this book. Go back over journal entries and reread your first few to get a sense of where you started and where you are now, reflecting on questions like these:

- How has your relationship with yourself changed?
- Are you experiencing greater expanded feelings in your day-to-day life?
- Do you feel a more profound sense of connection to yourself, your body, and your intuition?
- How have broadened perspectives opened you up to life?
- Has your experience of connection with others changed in some way?

Throughout your journey, your new superpowers have needed time to develop, which is perfect. Remember, the spiral nature of life is ever-present.

Everyone revisits old themes. Simply remember the awareness that you are at a higher level with it. You are constantly progressing on the spiral. Who you are today is the evolution of who you were just yesterday! There is a time and place to rest or focus on things other than your evolution. Feel into where you are with this and honor wherever you find yourself.

You may have had an affinity for some exercises and not others. This is excellent feedback for yourself. I encourage you to go back and integrate those other practices into your daily meditations. This is a signal of places that need some focus and Love with patience and perseverance.

Wherever you find yourself on your greater path, and however you have interacted with this book, I am grateful for your willingness to better yourself and, by extension, better the world.

## How to Get More Grounded in Your Evolution

One of the best ways to maintain your progress is to keep up your daily meditations. Utilize some of this book's practices and add new ones you find from other sources or gain through intuitive learning.

One of the most essential touchstones you can stay in contact with is the pink chamber of your heart space. As you continue to develop your relationship with this aspect of yourself, it will stabilize and integrate. These are the most important pieces to continue to work with. Secondly, remember the function of your physical heart and heart chakra during everyday life. Continue to integrate experiences as they happen through this technology.

To assist integration further, you can develop a new daily meditation that brings the presence of this higher aspect into each of the chakras we have worked with. First, bring it from the heart to the solar plexus. Tune in to how it interacts with this chakra. How do the aspects of your expanded self relate to the themes of the solar plexus? Journal about these connections. Work this way with the sacral, root, knees, and feet. You are now creating your expansions with your inner guidance system and previous experience.

Evolution passed the activation you have achieved is a choice. You are the creator of your human experience. Although now, you will work alongside spirit to achieve your further evolutions. When many more on the planet have achieved their heart activation, it will be time for the masses to choose further expanded openings.

It is a choice because you may be content with your current achievements. We are not meant to reach enlightenment in every incarnation. Enlightenment has not been our goal. There are many levels of remembering. It depends on what experience you want and how you move with the collective. We will all get where we need to be. Are you enjoying the process more?

There are spiritual processes to go through at each subsequent step beyond the heart, resulting in more awareness and the activation of higher functions. Just a reminder that these advancements surpass the heart activation that humanity is currently moving toward. This book covers the most significant evolution in our lifetime for the progress on the planet.

When you feel you are ready, evolve your practice. Seek other resources that resonate with your spiritual path, which may or may not include the next book in this series (which is yet to be written). However, keep in mind this quote from an unknown source:

*If you always have a guide, you will always be lost. If you always have a mentor, you will always be a student. If you always have a healer, you will always be broken.*

While it is common to seek guidance at the beginning of your spiritual awakening, there comes a point where you need less external guidance and can rely more on the internal guidance system that you have developed. That is part of the purpose of this book: to bring you to a place where you can create and understand your reality through the gift of your individual perspective, then use your inner guidance to determine how to proceed.

This book has been an offering to get you where you can find your way through to your truth in the deepest recesses of your heart. It is a balance because we will always need the reflections of others to grow and evolve. This is the beauty of having a separate human experience—the paradox of being whole on your own and utilizing your experiences with others to show you where your edges of evolution are.

My deepest gratitude to you for having this experience with me. Blessings on your continued journey.

# Glossary

Appreciation: The recognition of the quality, value, significance, or magnitude of people and things; a sensitive awareness; increase in value.

Ayurveda: A thousands-of-years-old system of medicine that originated in India. It seeks to integrate the physical body with the mind and spirit. In this book, we mainly considered the nutritional wisdom of this system.

Awareness: One of the aspects we are cultivating in this book. Awareness is your attention and understanding without words or thoughts.

Beingness: The experience of feeling the truth of who you are beyond this human experience. Accessed initially by emptying the mind and heart space with breathwork and meditation while also being open and receptive. Often felt in the heart space and perceived as being gold light.

Collective Unconscious: Carl Jung's theory of a shared mental field with shared concepts.

Consciousness: An awareness of internal and external existence. The expansion of consciousness is related to the expanded sense of self within your life and the universe.

Contracting Emotion: Emotional contraction occurs when we feel "negative" feelings like anger, sadness, grief, and frustration. This relates to the way polarity is necessary for all creation. This is the negative pole. See its counterpart, expansion.

Density: The unresolved emotional issues and beliefs that must be cleared in order to evolve.

Drama Triangle: A model of human interaction developed by Stephen B. Karpman, used to describe the dynamics of victimhood and the creation of conflict between people.

Duality Consciousness: A level of consciousness based on the false premise of one's disconnection from self, others, nature, and the universe at large. This perception limits all one's decisions and understanding of reality.

Epigenetics: Features that occur "on top of" your DNA impact how your genes are read, either up-regulating or down-regulating. This causes physiological changes and is part of your body's innate homeostatic system.

Ego (Separate Self): Left-brain cognition rooted in a separate sense of self and this incarnation's specific personality. Also, related to the solar plexus chakra and the I AM presence.

Essence: "The intrinsic or indispensable quality or qualities that serve to characterize or identify something; the most important aspect of something" (*The American Heritage Dictionary of the English Language*, 5th Edition).

Expanding Emotion: This can be felt in the body as a sense of freedom, Love, or joy. After an emotional contraction has been integrated, the growth or spark of insight that comes as an expansion. It also relates to polarity, as it is necessary for all creation. This is the positive pole. See its counterpart, contraction.

Experience: Your individual understanding of reality is built through perceptions and beliefs and their applications in the world and the situations you create. These then feed your perceptions and beliefs.

Fractal: Repeating geometry at different levels of magnification. Self-similar.

Freeze-Frame Technique (FFT): HeartMath Institute's technique to bring in more emotional coherence during a trigger.

Hormone: *Chapter 1*—a chemical messenger evolved through behavior and physiology to aid in procreation and survival. *Chapter 3*—a chemical substance secreted by glands in the brain and nervous system that drives human experience. In the immature human, the lack of hormones leads to a cycle of contracting emotions and experiences without tools to navigate and evolve. The beginning of maturation is the circulation of more hormones though our mammalian technology of emotions. *Chapter 5*— the connection between perceived experiences of the nervous system and the secretion of hormones directed by the nervous system. *Chapter 9*—the vehicle through which self-union occurs, and the attainment of maturation.

Homeostasis: The core principle for the body of all living things to self-regulate and continue life.

Intuition: When you know or understand something without proof through the use of senses beyond the mundane.

love (*lowercase*): *Chapter 1*—a primitive adaptation of the human hormone system that drives behavior for procreation, child-rearing, and cooperation with others in groups. *Chapter 3*—the creation of health in the body through connection with yourself, others, and the wider world. *Chapter 5*—having balanced emotions and access to the operations of both sides of the brain.

Love (*capitalized*): *Chapter 7*—an omnipresent force and potential within the universe, incarnated in your heart space, either accessed or not. *Chapter 9*—a conscious intelligence that is both the vehicle of evolution (spirit/masculine principle) and the material being evolved (form/feminine principle). It is each pole and the interplay between poles. Love is that which is creating all and all that is created. Love manifests form.

Incarnation: your current human embodiment.

Macrocosm/Microcosm: The existence of structural similarities at different scales. For example, a comparison of the eye of a human (small level), the Helix Nebula (large level) shows a similarity. Related to the concept of fractals.

Maturation: An evolution of the hormonal system, acquired by releasing density and cultivating higher-frequency feelings of gratitude, admiration, optimism, and Love.

Perception: The process of perceiving or becoming aware of something.

Polarity: Two-dimensional tools to create in the third dimension. Examples of polarity include light and dark, good and bad, and masculine and feminine principles.

Personal Reality: The cataloged beliefs an individual has about the world around them that greatly impact their experience.

Quantum Leap: An awareness that becomes a conscious choice to make an evolution that would otherwise have taken more time.

Senses: Nervous system biology evolved to help an individual perceive and experience the world and keep them safe.

Spiral Path: The theory that evolutions (including personal and individual evolutions) occur in a spiral-like experience. As you circle around and up, you may revisit old themes but at a higher level of mastery. It can sometimes be frustrating because you do not perceive the higher octave attained.

Spiritual Bypass: The tendency to use spiritual ideas and practices to sidestep or avoid facing unresolved emotional issues, psychological wounds, and unfinished developmental tasks.

True Essence (True Self): Your complete nature beyond the human experience or human form. Related to beingness.

Unbalanced Separate Self: Unbalanced ego that seeks outside the self to determine who the self is. Often including more contracting or negative feelings about previous experiences that many people try to push away or ignore.

# Suggested Readings and Tools

This section has been included to give you extra support for your journey and additional context for the material in this book. Many are pivotal writings that had a heavy influence on my writing of this book. I encourage you to explore them if you feel drawn to them.

*Prakriti: Your Ayurvedic Constitution* by Dr. Robert E. Svoboda

*The Chakras and Their Functions* by Master Choa Kok Sui

*Initiation* Hosted by Matías de Stephano on Gaia.com

*Serpent Rising: The Kundalini Compendium* by Neven Paar

*The Presence of the Past* by Rupert Sheldrake

*Advanced Spiritual Intimacy* by Stuart Sovatsky

*Words from the Soul* by Stuart Sovatsky

*New Brain, New World* by Erick Hoffmann

*Universal and Nature Intelligence Cards, #1 and #2* by Janine Thorpe available at Janine Thorpe.com

# References

In order of appearance in each chapter

## Chapter 1

Longrich, Nicolas R. "The Origin and Evolution of Love," *Encyclopedia Britannica.*
https://www.britannica.com/story/the-origin-and-evolution-oflove

Hoffman, E. A., and Rowe, T. B. "Jurassic Stem-Mammal Perinates and the Origin of Mammalian Reproduction and Growth." *Nature* 561(2018): 104–108.

Wardecker, B. M., Smith, L. K., Edelstein, RS, et al. "Intimate Relationships Then and Now: How Old Hormonal Processes Are Influenced by Our Modern Psychology." *Adaptive Human Behavior and Physiology* 1 (2015): 150–176.

Kleinman, D. G. "Monogamy in Mammals." *The Quarterly Review of Biology* 52 (1977): 39–69.

Wobber, V. H., Lipson, S, et al. "Different Ontogenetic Patterns of Testosterone Production Reflect Divergent Male Reproductive Strategies in Chimpanzees and Bonobos." *Physiology and Behavior* 116–117 (2013): 44–53.

Hohmann, G., and Fruth, B. "Intra- and Inter-Sexual Aggression by Bonobos in the Context of Mating." *Behavior* 140 (2003): 1389–1414.

Slatcher, R. B., Mehta, P. H., and Josephs, RA. "Testosterone and Self-Reported Dominance Interact to Influence Human Mating Behavior." *Social Physiological and Personality Science* 2 (2011): 531–539.

Sobolewski, M. E., Brown, J. L., and Mitani, J. C. "Territoriality, Tolerance, and Testosterone in Wild Chimpanzees." *Animal Behavior* 84 (2012): 1469–1474.

Edelstein, R. S., van Anders, S. M., Chopik, W. J., et al. "Dyadic Associations Between Testosterone and Relationship Quality in Couples." *Hormones and Behavior* 65 (2014): 401–407.

Burnham, T. C., Chapman, J. F., Gray, and P. B., et al. "Men in Committed, Romantic Relationships Have Lower Testosterone." *Hormones and Behavior* 44 (2003): 119–122.

Archer, J., Graham-Kevan, N., and Davies, M. "Testosterone and Aggression: A Reanalysis of Book Starzyk and Quinsey's (2001) study." *Aggression and Violent Behavior* 10 (2005): 241–261.

Edelstein, R. S., Kean, E. L., and Chopik, W. J. "Women with Avoidant Attachment Styles Show Attenuated Estradiol Response to Emotionally Intimate Stimuli." *Hormones and Behavior* 61 (2012): 167–175.

Bouissou, M.F. "Effects of Estrogen Treatment on Dominance Relationships in Cows." *Hormones and Behavior* 24 (1990): 376–387.

Michael, R. P., and Zumpe, D. "A Review of Hormonal Factors Influencing the Sexual and Aggressive Behavior of Macaques." *American Journal of Primatology* 30 (1993): 213–241.

deCatanzaro, D., Khan, A., Berger, RG., and Lewis, E. "Exposure to Developing Females Induces Polyuria, Polydipsia, and Altered Urinary Levels of Creatinine, 17 Best-Estradiol, and Testosterone in Adult Mice (Mus Musculus)." *Hormones and Behavior* 55 (2009): 240–247.

Antonio Cabrera, E., and Paredes, R. G. "Effects of Chronic Estradiol or Testosterone Treatment Upon Sexual Behavior in Sexually Sluggish Male Rats." Pharmacology, Biochemistry, and Behavior 101 (2012): 336–341.

Ogawa, S., Chester, A. E., Hewitt, S. C., et al. "Abolition of Male Sexual Behavior in Mice Lacking Estrogen Receptors Alpha and Beta." Proceedings of the National Academy of Sciences 97 (2000): 14737–14741.

Bowlby, J. "Attachment Theory and Its Therapeutic Implications." *Adolescent Psychiatry* 6 (1978): 5–33.

Simpson, J. A., and Besky, J. "Attachment Theory Within a Modern Evolutionary Framework." In *Handbook of Attachment: Theory, Research and Clinical Applications*, 2nd ed., edited by J. Cassidy and P. R. Shaver, 131–157. New York: Guilford Press, 2008.

Michelini, L. C. "Oxytocin in the NTS." *Annals of the New York Academy of Sciences* 940 (2001): 206–220.

Uvnäs-Moberg, K., Handlin, L., and Peterson, M. "Self-Soothing Behaviors with Particular Reference to Oxytocin Release Induced by Non-Noxious Sensory Stimulation." *Front Psychol* 5 (2015): 1529. doi: 10.3389/fpsyg.2014.01529.

Sheldrake, R. *The Presence of the Past: Morphic Resonance and the Memory of Nature.* Park Street Press, 2012.

McDougall, W. "Fourth Report on a Lamarckian Experiment." *British Journal of Psychology* 28 (1938): 321–345.

Stephano, Matías de. "The Universe Within." The Four Winds Society. November 27, 2023.

# Chapter 2

Nestor, J. *Breath: The New Science of a Lost Art.* Penguin, 2020.

Stephano, Matías de. "The Universe Within." The Four Winds Society. November 27, 2023.

# Chapter 3

van Honk, J., Terburg, D., and Bos, P.A. "Further Notes on Testosterone as a Social Hormone." *Trends in Cognitive Sciences* 15, no. 7 (2011): 291–292.

Amin, Z., Canli, T., and Epperson, C. N. "Effect of Estrogen-Serotonin Interactions on Mood and Cognition." *Behav Cogn Neurosci Rev* 4, no. 1 (2005): 43–58. doi: 10.1177/1534582305277152.

Tom, N., and Assinder, S. "Oxytocin in Health and Disease." *The International Journal of Biochemistry and Cell Biology* 42, no. 2 (2010): 202–205.

Follesa, P., Serra, M., Cagetti, E., Pisu, M.G., Porta, S., Floris, S., et al. "Allopregnanolone Synthesis in Cerebellar Granule Cells: Roles in Regulation of GABAA Receptor Expression and Function During Progesterone Treatment and Withdrawal." *Molecular Pharmacology* 57, no. 6 (2000): 1262–1270.

Harvard Health Publishing. "Dopamine: The Pathway to Pleasure." Accessed December 8, 2022. https://www.health.harvard.edu/mind-and-mood/dopamine-the-pathway-to-pleasure.

Daly, J. W., Holmén, J., and Fredholm, B. B. "Is Caffeine Addictive? The Most Widely Used Psychoactive Substance in the World Affects Same Parts of the Brain as Cocaine." *Lakartidningen* 95, no. 51–52 (1998): 5878–5883.

Casagrande, C. "Dopamine and the Kidney in Heart Failure." *Herz* 16, no. 2 (1991): 102–115.

Underland, L. J., Mark, E., et al. "The Impact of Dopamine on Insulin Secretion in Healthy Controls." *Indian J Crit Care Med* 22, no. 4 (2018): 209–213.

Wood, P. B. "Role of Central Dopamine in Pain and Analgesia." *Expert Rev Neurother* 8, no. 5 (2008): 781–797. doi: 10.1586/14737175.8.5.781. PMID: 18457535.

Lee, S. "Opioids and Universal Experience of Addiction by Dr. Gabor Maté." Dr. Gabor Maté, May 8, 2017. https://drgabormate. com/opioids-universal-experience-addiction/.

Wasserman, A., et al. "Oxytocin Promotes Epicardial Cell Activation and Heart Regeneration After Cardiac Injury." *Front. Cell Dev. Biol.* 10 (2022). https://doi.org/10.3389/fcell.2022.985298.

Erdman, S. E. "Oxytocin and the Microbiome." *Current Opinion in Endocrine and Metabolic Research* 19 (2021): 8–14.

Blevins, J. E., and Ho, J. M. "Role of Oxytocin Signaling in the Regulation of Body Weight." *Rev Endocr Metab Disord* 14, no. 4 (2013): 311–329. doi: 10.1007/s11154-013-9260-x.

Lei, C. L., Laplante, D. P., and King, S. "Prenatal Maternal Stress and Epigenetics: Review of the Human Research." *Current Molecular Biology Reports* 2, no. 1 (2016): 16–25.

Church, D. *Genie in Your Genes: Epigenetic Medicine and the New Biology of Intention.* Hay House, 2018.

Crum, A. J., and Langer, E. J. "Mind-Set Matters: Exercise and the Placebo Effect." *Psychological Science* 18, no. 2 (2007): 165–171.

Dossey, L. "Prayer and Medical Science: A Commentary on the Prayer Study by Harris et al and a Response to Critics." *Archives of Internal Medicine* 160, no. 12 (2000): 1735–1738.

Ironson, G., Stuetzle, R., and Fletcher, M. A. "An Increase in Religiousness/Spirituality Occurs After HIV Diagnosis and Predicts Slower Disease Progression Over Four Years in People with HIV." *Journal of General Internal Medicine* 21, no. 5 (2006): S62–S68.

Fetterman, J. L., and Ballinger, S. W. "Mitochondrial Genetics Regulate Nuclear Gene Expression Through Metabolites." (2019) *Proceedings of the National Academy of Sciences* 116, no. 32: 15763–157.

LeDoux, J. "Rethinking the Emotional Brain." *Neuron* 73, no. 4 (2012): 653–676.

Gouin, J. P., Kiecolt-Glaser, J. K., et al. "The Influence of Anger Expression on Wound Healing." *Brain Behav Immun* 22, no. 5 (2008): 699–708.

Marcus, G. *The Birth of the Mind: How a Tiny Number of Genes Creates the Complexity of Human Thought.* Basic Books, 2014.

Zacks, J. *Flicker: Your Brain on Movies.* 1st ed. Oxford University Press, 2014.

Gottman, T. *Principia Amoris: The New Science of Love.* 1st ed. Routledge, 2014.

Emmons, R. A., McCullough, M. E. "Counting Blessings Versus Burdens: An Experimental Investigation of Gratitude and Subjective Well-Being in Daily Life." *J Pers Soc Psychol* 84, no. 2 (2003): 377–389. doi: 10.1037//0022-3514.84.2.377. PMID: 12585811.

Barraza, J. A., Zak, P. J. "Empathy Toward Strangers Triggers Oxytocin Release and Subsequent Generosity." *Annals of the New York Academy of Sciences* 1167 (2009): 182–189.

Stephano, Matías de. "The Universe Within." The Four Winds Society. November 27, 2023.

## Chapter 4

Stephano, Matías de. "The Universe Within." The Four Winds Society. November 27, 2023.

## Chapter 5

Heyes, C. "New Thinking: The Evolution of Human Cognition." *Philos Trans R Soc Lond B Biol Sci* 367, no. 1599 (2012): 2091–6. doi: 10.1098/rstb.2012.0111.

Hoffmann, E. *New Brain, New World.* Hay House, 2012.

Yong, E. "Not a Hug Hormone: Fish Version of Oxytocin Acts as Social Spotlight." *Science*, National Geographic, May 4, 2021. https://www.nationalgeographic.com/science/article/fish-oxytocin -isotocin-social-spotlight.

Janov, A. *The Primal Scream.* Dell Publishing, 1970.

"Can Consciousness Exist Outside of the Brain?" *Psychology Today.* https://www.psychologytoday.com/us/blog/think-well/201906/ can-consciousness-exist-outside-the-brain.

Garland, T., Zhao, M., and Saltzman, W. "Hormones and the Evolution of Complex Traits: Insights from Artificial Selection on Behavior." *Integr Comp Biol* 52, no. 2 (2016): 207–224.

"Dogs Have a Conscience Too." *Neuroscience News*, December 8, 2015. https://neurosciencenews.com/self-aware-dog-psychology-3240/.

Jaynes, J. *The Origin of Consciousness in the Breakdown of the Bicameral Mind.* Boston, MA: Houghton Mifflin, 1976.

Sovatsky, S. *Words from the Soul.* State University of New York Press, Albany, NY: 1998.

L'Abate, L. "The Drama Triangle: An Attempt to Resurrect a Neglected Pathogenic Model in Family Therapy Theory and Practice." *The American Journal of Family Therapy* 37, no. 1 (2009): 1–11.

Welwood, J. "Principles of Inner Work: Psychological and Spiritual." *The Journal of Transpersonal Psychology* 16, no. 1 (1984).

Stephano, Matías de. "The Universe Within." The Four Winds Society. November 27, 2023.

## Chapter 6

Emmons, Robert. "Gratitude and the Science of Positive Psychology." UC Davis Faculty—Robert Emmons, 2002. emmons.faculty.ucdavis. edu/wp-content/uploads/sites/90/2015/08/2002_2-gratandsc.-of-pos_2002.pdf. Accessed October 31, 2023.

Stephano, Matías de. "The Universe Within." The Four Winds Society. November 27, 2023.

## Chapter 7

"Hormone (n.)." *Encyclopædia Britannica.* https://www.britannica.com/science/hormone.

Adam, J., et al. (STAR Collaboration). "Measurement of $e^+e^-$ Momentum and Angular Distributions from Linearly Polarized Photon Collisions." *Physical Review Letters* 127 (2021): 052302. DOI: 10.1103/physrevlett.127.052302.

"Collisions of Light Produce Matter/Antimatter from Pure Energy." *Brookhaven National Laboratory*, July 28, 2021. www.bnl.gov/newsroom/news.php?a=119023.

Heyes, C., et al. "Knowing Ourselves Together: The Cultural Origins of Metacognition." *Trends in Cognitive Sciences* 24, no. 5 (2020): 349–362.

McCraty, R., and Childre, D. *The Appreciative Heart: The Psychophysiology of Positive Emotions and Optimal Functioning*. Institute of HeartMath, Boulder Creek, CA; 2002.

Childre, D., and McCraty, R. "Psychophysiological Correlates of Spiritual Experience." *Biofeedback* 29, no. 4 (Winter 2001): 13-17.

Pearsall, Paul P. *The Heart's Code: Tapping the Wisdom and Power of Our Heart Energy*. National Geographic Books, 1999.

Stephano, Matías de. "The Universe Within." The Four Winds Society. November 27, 2023.

# Chapter 8

Stephano, Matías de. "The Universe Within." The Four Winds Society. November 27, 2023.

# Chapter 9

Sovatsky, Stuart. *Advanced Spiritual Intimacy: The Yoga of Deep Tantric Sensuality*. Simon and Schuster.

# Chapter 10

O'Malley, Liam. "What Is Unconditional Love?" *IONS*, 25 Aug. 2022, noetic.org/blog/what-is-unconditional-love.

# Chapter 11

Sovatsky, Stuart. *Advanced Spiritual Intimacy: The Yoga of Deep Tantric Sensuality*. Simon and Schuster.

www.ingramcontent.com/pod-product-compliance
Lightning Source LLC
Chambersburg PA
CBHW071150130626
46553CB00004B/1596